ENGLISH FOR INTERNATIONAL
TOURISM

IWONNA DUBICKA • MARGARET O'KEEFFE

CONTENTS

WORLD TOURISM

Grammar: present simple question forms
Vocabulary: tourism statistics
Professional skills: checking and confirming details
Case study: make the right booking

1 These are the top eight destinations for international tourism. What are the nationalities of people from these countries? Write the words in the correct group.

> ~~Australia~~   Britain   China   France   Germany
> Italy   Spain   USA

-n	-ian	-ish	-ese	other
Australian				

PRONUNCIATION

2)) **1.1** Listen to the countries and nationalities. Underline the main word stress. Practise the pronunciation.

Aus<u>tra</u>lia: Aus<u>tra</u>lian

3)) **1.2** Add the nationalities from these countries to the table above. Listen and check the pronunciation.

> Brazil   Canada   Greece   Ireland   India   Japan
> Kenya   Korea   Mexico   Norway   Poland   Portugal
> Russia   Thailand   The Netherlands   Turkey

4 Read this article about Chinese travellers and decide if the statements are true (T) or false (F). Correct the false statements.

1 The majority of outbound trips are to Asian destinations.   T / F

2 Half of outbound trips are to Europe and the USA.   T / F

3 Germany, France and Italy are the top destinations in Europe.   T / F

4 Chinese tourists generally like to spend money on luxury hotels.   T / F

5 Chinese tourists prefer independent travel.   T / F

Chinese travellers

China, with the biggest population in the world, is an important emerging market for international tourism. There are now more than 57 million outbound trips every year.

Most Chinese tourists, over 70 percent, go to Hong Kong and Macau. Of the rest, more than half stay in Asia – Japan, South Korea, and Thailand are among the other top destinations. Fewer than 10 percent go to Europe – particularly Germany, France and Italy – and the USA.

Many surveys conducted in these countries show that Chinese tourists' favourite activity is shopping, especially for luxury brands. Chinese tourists also spend more on tax-free shopping than visitors from other countries. In response to this demand, department stores in central Paris now have signs and services dedicated to Chinese shoppers.

Surveys also show that the Chinese typically travel in large tour groups of 30–40 people and they prefer to save money on food and accommodation in order to spend more in the shops.

Visiting historic monuments is the second favourite activity. The French attractions of the Louvre, the Eiffel Tower and Versailles Palace are the most popular with Chinese travellers.

5 One word or phrase in each group is <u>not</u> part of the tourism sector. Which sector does it belong to?

1 Accommodation: campsite, art gallery, bed and breakfast, motel _____

2 Transportation: airline, taxi, golf, tram _____

3 Attractions: museum, zoo, business convention, theme park _____

4 Food and beverage: car hire, café, restaurant, pizzeria _____

5 Recreation and entertainment: skiing, trekking, cycling, bistro _____

6 Events and conferences: Olympic Games, tennis tournament, hostel, music festival _____

6 Put the questions (1–6) in the correct order. Then match the questions and answers (a–f).

1 museum / the / Louvre / is / where

_____ ?

2 visitors / does / how / museum / get / many / the

_____ ?

3 big / Louvre's / collection / how / the / is

_____ ?

4 attraction / the / is / what / top

_____ ?

5 does / visit / how / to / it / cost / the / museum / much _____?

6 long / tour / guided / is / how / the

_____ ?

a It contains more than 380,000 objects and exhibits 35,000 works of art from prehistory to the 19th century.

b *Mona Lisa* by Leonardo da Vinci.

c The introductory tour lasts 90 minutes and it is available in English.

d It's in the centre of Paris, France on the right bank of the river Seine.

e Entry is 10 euros for the permanent collection. It is free to visitors under 18.

f There are over 8 million visitors a year. It is the most visited art museum in the world.

7 Françoise Martin works at the Louvre. Complete the interview questions with <u>one to three</u> words.

1 _____ your job?

I'm a Visitor Service Officer at the Louvre.

2 _____ staff _____ the museum have?

It employs 2,000 people. Over half are security officers.

3 _____ some of the typical questions visitors ask you?

'Where's the Mona Lisa?' 'Is the museum open yet?' 'Where are the toilets? '

4 _____ a good time to visit?

Early in the week in the morning – the museum opens at 9 a.m. but it's closed on Tuesdays.

5 _____ you work at the weekends?

Quite a lot. Usually twice a month.

6 _____ like most about your job?

Smiles and thank-yous from satisfied visitors.

PRONUNCIATION

1))) **1.3** **Put the other letters of the alphabet in the correct column. Listen and check.**

/eɪ/	/iː/	/e/	/aɪ/	/əʊ/	/uː/	/ɑː/
say	please	sent	I	phone	do	card
A	B C	___ ___	___	___	___	___
___	___ ___	___ ___			___	
___	___ ___	___ ___			___	
___	___ ___	___				

2))) **1.4** **Listen to a customer booking train tickets and complete the information.**

Outward date: ¹_____

Departure time	From	To	Arr	Duration
²_____	London Euston	Manchester Piccadilly	³_____	2.07

Return date: ⁴_____

Departure time	From	To	Arr	Duration
⁵_____	Manchester Piccadilly	London Euston	⁶_____	2.12

Price 1x Adult: ⁷_____

Quantity: 2

Total price: ⁸_____

3))) **Listen again and complete what the booking agent says. Use one or two words in each space. Practise saying the phrases using polite intonation.**

1 _____ or return?

2 Do you want to travel _____ or return to London?

3 _____ you want to travel?

4 _____ two return tickets from London Euston to Manchester Piccadilly.

5 The cheapest _____ is eighty pounds twenty return.

6 Would you like a _____ ?

7 6 a.m. or _____ ?

8 _____ you like to pay for that?

5 **Complete these expressions for checking and confirming with one word. Listen again if necessary to check your answers.**

1 Can I _____ your name, please?

2 Could you _____ your name for me?

3 Can I have your credit card _____ ?

4 I'll just read that _____ to you.

5 Sorry, sorry, I _____ 9–1–8–7.

6 Can you _____ that, please?

4))) **1.5** **Listen to the tourist in Exercise 2 making a telephone call. Complete the booking details.**

Matchday VIP package

Watch the match from excellent seats near to the Directors' Box. Enjoy this legendary team's entertaining football. Offer includes: match tickets, hot and cold snacks, match programme, free gift.

Match: Manchester United vs Arsenal

Date and time:	¹_____
VIP package per person	²_____
VIP name(s):	³_____
Credit card details:	⁴_____
Email:	⁵_____
Contact our hospitality team on:	⁶_____

1 Look at these advertisements for holiday packages in the USA and answer the questions. Write OR for Orlando and AL for Alaska, or OR / AL for both. Which holiday package(s) ...

1 include(s) transport at the destinations? _____

2 include(s) some meals? _____

3 doesn't include accommodation? _____

4 is only available in summer months? _____

5 include(s) flights? _____

US Fly-drive Holidays*

Gives you the freedom and flexibility to go where you want, when you want.
Call our experts on 0266 7797 2000 and we'll design your perfect holiday.

Orlando

Home to the best theme parks in the world.
7, 10 and 14-night fly-drives from just £499 (adult prices).
Buy Orlando One-Pass from us before you go. The One-Pass gives you 14 days unlimited admission to all the top theme parks and attractions.

Alaska Tour

Enjoy this 12-night fly-drive tour: glaciers, national parks, wildlife and beautiful towns and villages.
Tour departs daily from 21 May–04 September.
Included: hotel accommodation, breakfast, road maps.

Not included: excursions and entrance tickets to national park.

* All of our fly-drive holidays include return flights and car hire for the duration of your stay.

2))) 1.6 Listen to a customer booking her holiday and complete the form.

Reservation

Type of holiday: Orlando Fly-Drive
Departing from: London Gatwick
Returning from: Orlando Sanford
Number of nights: [1]_____
Out Date: [2] _____
Return Date: [3]_____
Price: [4]_____ adult fare
     [5]_____ child fare
Number of Adults: 2
Name(s): [6]_____
Number of Children:
Name(s): [7]_____
Note: Email client information about
[8]_____

---

3))) 1.7 Listen to a later phone call with the customer and correct the email confirming the changes to the booking. There are <u>six</u> changes to the booking.

From:	**Yolanda@wgtravel.com**
To:	**Odonnell@omail.com**
Subject:	**Reservation Orlando fly-drive**

Dear Mrs O'Donnell

Thank you for booking with WG Travel. I am writing to confirm your reservation. Here are the details we discussed on the telephone today:

Flights: London Gatwick (LGW) to Orlando Sanford (SFB)

Departure date: Saturday 4th August at 09.10

Return date: Tuesday 14th August at 05.30

Total duration: 10 nights

Fly-drive only – no accommodation

Not included: Car insurance

Total price: £4,133

Payment made by credit card. Thank you.

Please find attached more details about the flights, car hire and villa.

We wish you and your family a wonderful holiday.

Best regards

Yolanda Squires

2 JOBS IN TOURISM

UNIT MENU

Grammar: present simple and present continuous
Vocabulary: working conditions, qualities and skills, hotel jobs
Professional skills: categories in a CV
Case study: covering letter, choose the right person for the job

1 **Look at the definitions and complete the crossword with jobs in travel and tourism.**

Across →

2 person who carries a guest's luggage to or from the room

4 hotel employee responsible for giving advice and additional services to guests

8 person who serves at tables in a restaurant

9 person responsible for serving food and drinks, and looking after passengers on a plane

10 employee of a hotel who cleans and maintains rooms and public spaces

Down ↓

1 another name for the front desk clerk of a hotel

3 someone who sells or arranges trips or tours for customers

5 professional cook

6 person who takes visitors on tours of sites, cities, or in nature

7 person whose job it is to tell jokes, sing and entertain people

2 **Which job does not relate to each category? Which sector does it belong to?**

1 Accommodation: bellboy, ski instructor, campsite manager, front desk agent _____

2 Transportation: coach driver, flight attendant, events manager, cruise director _____

3 Attractions: cloakroom attendant, site manager, concierge, theme park supervisor _____

4 Food and beverage: museum guide, waiter, kitchen assistant, café manager _____

5 Recreation and entertainment: children's entertainer, executive chef, entertainments manager, outdoor adventure guide _____

6 Events and conferences: travel agent, conference organizer, pilot, exhibitor _____

3 **))) 2.1** **Read about these jobs in tourism and complete the personal qualities needed. The first letters are given. Listen and check your answers.**

1 If you want to work as a holiday rep, or resort representative, you need to be outgoing, enthusiastic, helpful, *fle_____* and have a *pro_____* appearance.

2 A housekeeper has to be *ha_____-w_____*, a good team worker, *ef_____* and also a bit of a perfectionist.

3 It's important that a restaurant manager is *or_____*, good at managing a team, and feels *pas_____* about food.

4 If you want to work for a children's attraction, you should be *res_____* but also fun-loving and *enter_____* and, most importantly, you have to like children.

5 A good tour guide is *enth_____*, patient, *com_____* and a 'people-person'.

PRONUNCIATION

4))) **2.2** Put the verbs in the correct group according to the pronunciation of the –s at the end of the verb in the 3rd person singular. Listen and check your answers.

> ~~books~~ checks ~~closes~~ communicates ~~deals~~
> does gives helps makes organizes
> plans prepares recommends serves
> specializes supervises works

/z/	/ɪz/	/s/
dea<u>ls</u>	clos<u>es</u>	book<u>s</u>

5 Complete these sentences about people who work in tourism using the correct form of the present continuous. Use contractions.

1 Yuetung is a concierge in a hotel in Macau. Last week she worked in the afternoon but this week she_____ (work) in the morning. At the moment some guests are asking her for information about the local attractions and her phone_____ (ring).

2 Pawel is a resort manager in a holiday centre. He works six days a week all the year. He_____ (have) a meeting now with some suppliers. They_____ (give) a presentation on new equipment for the water park.

3 Afon is a student but in the summer she works as an entertainments manager in a seaside resort in Wales, UK. At the moment she_____ (plan) the children's activities and she_____ (ask) the magician to include some new tricks in his show.

4 Derek works as a freelance events manager. He usually works three or four days a week. This month he_____ (prepare) stands for an exhibition in Brazil. At the moment he_____ (supervise) the design and printing of publicity material.

6 Look again at the people in Exercise 5. Match the people (1–4) to the type of work they do (a–d).

a seasonal work_____

b shift work_____

c part-time work_____

d full-time work_____

7))) **2.3** Listen to Jenny Butler, the executive chef at the Bouvier hotel. Why is she very busy this week? Tick (✓) the correct alternative (a, b or c).

a The hotel is organizing lunch for 350 guests and she's planning the menu with a chef. _____

b The hotel is catering for a wedding with 150 guests and she's checking the fish order. _____

c The hotel has a conference dinner for 450 guests and she's making sure everything is OK. _____

8))) Listen again and complete the sentences about what Jenny does and what she's doing at the moment. Use contractions where possible.

1 I_____ for the Bouvier Hotel and I_____ responsible for the chefs and kitchen staff.

2 At the moment I_____ the menu for a special dinner.

3 The hotel_____ a conference this week and there_____ a lot of guests.

4 I_____ to the restaurant manager to make sure everything_____ perfectly.

5 The food and beverage manager_____ if another supplier can deliver the fish.

6 It's great when a waiter_____ me our guests_____their meal.

1 Match the headings to the different sections (1–8) of Afon's CV.

> Additional information   Personal details   Education and qualifications
> Interests   Profile   References   Voluntary experience   Work experience

Afon Hali Jones

1 _____

Address:	24, Chester Road, Wrexham, Clwyd, LL15 4QU, UK
Home tel. no:	+ 44 (0)1745 463 218
Mobile number:	+44 (0)7950 694207
Email:	afon.hjones@wworld.co.uk

2 _____

An outgoing and professional tourism (i)_____ with experience in different areas including entertainment and (ii)_____, and food and beverages. Looking to put into practice academic ability and (iii)_____ experience in the entertainment and leisure sector.

3 _____

2010–present   BA in Tourism Management, University of Clwyd
Specializing in entertainments and leisure
Work experience at the Theatre Clwyd and the Leisure Centre in Llandudno

2008–2010   Mold College
3 A-levels
English Language (A)
Business Studies (B)
French (B)

2002–2008   Mold Secondary School
8 GCSEs Grades A–C

4 _____

July–Aug. 2013   Entertainment Manager, Llandudno holiday centre

July–Aug. 2012   Assistant Entertainment Manager, Llandudno holiday centre
Organizing evening entertainment: karaoke, games and a children's magic show
Planning sports activities, competitions, and day trips
Presenting sports events and shows
Coordinating schedules with centre staff, tour guides and entertainers
Giving local information and advice to customers
Maintaining excellent levels of customer satisfaction in the peak holiday period

2010-2012   Student Café Supervisor, University of Clwyd
Serving customers and maintaining high levels of customer service
Managing the café in line with health and safety regulations
Training new café staff
Planning and organizing staff rotas

5 _____

2008-2009   Volunteer, Llandudno Visitor Centre
Giving local information to visitors
Booking tickets and accommodation
Assisting tour guides and interpreting on excursions

6 _____

IT skills: Word, Excel, PowerPoint, internet and email.
Languages: fluent in English and Welsh; Advanced Greek and Intermediate French
Full, clean driving licence

7 _____

Sports: captain of the women's University hockey team; taekwondo
Travel and music – singing, guitar

8 _____

Available on request

2 Complete gaps (i)–(iii) in Afon's profile at the start of her CV. Choose the correct option (a, b or c).

(i)   **a** graduate   **b** specialist   **c** consultant
(ii)   **a** sporty   **b** leisure   **c** hobbies
(iii) **a** profession   **b** qualifications   **c** work

3 What is the aim of a profile statement in a CV? Tick (✓) the correct alternative (a, b or c).

a to show what job the candidate is applying for _____

b to give details about a candidate's employment record _____

c to summarize a candidate's experience and background _____

1 Read about four tourism jobs. Match the job titles (a-d) to the descriptions (1–3). One job is <u>not</u> used.

a Events manager   **c** Resort manager

b Entertainments and leisure manager   **d** Concierge

Job 1 _____

This person helps to provide a fun experience in a purpose-built holiday centre. He/She trains new staff, and checks that tours and entertainment services are well-organized. His/Her team are usually the first people to receive questions from guests, and they inform visitors about where to drink, eat, or shop. He/She supervises the onsite entertainment, which can include children's shows and sports activities.

Job 2 _____

This person is responsible for management, training and staff motivation. He/She supervises staff and makes sure all transfers, welcome meetings and evening entertainment go well. He/She trains the reps in a holiday centre so that they can answer visitor's questions on the area. There are also administrative duties, for example checking weekly accounts and meetings.

Job 3 _____

This person's job is to serve the needs of guests in a hotel or resort. He/She usually gives information about tours and attractions, transportation and directions. This person often books tickets and recommends tours. The job involves communicating with guests, both face to face and on the telephone.

2 Afon is applying for job position 1. Complete her cover letter to Sunnyside resorts. The first letter of each word is given.

Dear Sir/Madam,

I am ¹ w_____ to apply for the position of Entertainments manager. Please find ² a_____ a copy of my CV.

I am very interested in working ³ f_____ Sunnyside resorts in Halkidiki, Greece because I am ⁴ p_____ about entertainment.

I am currently ⁵ s_____ for a degree in Tourism management at the University of Clywd in North Wales. I have ⁶ e_____ as an Entertainments manager because I have worked at a resort for two summers. At Llandudno I am ⁷ r_____ for organizing entertainment, for example, karaoke, children's shows and sport activities.

I believe I am ⁸ o_____, hard-working and enthusiastic. In addition, I work well in a ⁹ t_____. As you can ¹⁰ s_____ from my CV, I also speak English, Welsh, Greek and some French.

I ¹¹ l_____ forward to hearing from you.

Yours ¹² f_____,

Afon Hali Jones

Afon Hali Jones

3))) 2.4   Listen to extracts from the interview with Afon and tick (✓) the questions the interviewer asks.

1 Do you have any experience as an entertainments manager? _____

2 Can you tell me about your studies? _____

3 What are your responsibilities there? _____

4 Could you give me some examples? _____

5 Can you describe your negative qualities? _____

6 What kind of qualities does an entertainments manager need? _____

7 Do you work well in a team? _____

8 What do you know about Sunnyside resorts? _____

4)))   Listen again and complete some of Afon's answers.

1 I've worked as an entertainments manager for two _____ in a seaside _____ in Llandudno.

2 I _____ and _____ entertainment for both adults and kids.

3 I'm _____ and outgoing, and I'm a good team _____.

3 VISITOR CENTRES

UNIT MENU

Grammar: comparative and superlative forms
Vocabulary: visitor information centres (VICs), adjectives
Professional skills: dealing with enquiries
Case study: improve a service

1 **Read the information about VisitBrussels tourist office and answer the tourist's questions.**

1 Where is the tourist information centre? _____

2 What are the opening hours on Sundays? _____

3 What does it cost to book a hotel? _____

4 How much does the Brussels Card cost for two days? _____

5 What public transport is included with the card? _____

VisitBrussels

At VisitBrussels our friendly team help you **make the most of** your visit. Our office is in the medieval Grand-Place, the central square in the heart of the city. We open every day from 9 a.m. to 6 p.m. We provide information to help you **see the sights**, local events and exhibitions. We can help you plan **day trips** to other charming cities in Belgium. We can also reserve accommodation for you free of charge. Alternatively, use our website to plan your trip. You can also buy the products in our e-shop.

You can buy the Brussels Card here. Choose from a 24h (€24), 48h (€34) or 72h (€40) card and get:

• free **admission** to over 30 museums

• **unlimited**, free travel on trams, buses and metro all over the city

• a free city map

• discount **vouchers** for bars, restaurants and shops.

2 **Read the website again and match the words in bold with their definitions (1–6).**

1 visits to places where you go and come back on the same day _____

2 take full advantage of _____

3 visit the famous, interesting places _____

4 tickets that can be used instead of money _____

5 cost of entrance to a building or event _____

6 unrestricted, so that you can go where you like as often as you like _____

3 **))) 3.1** **Listen to the interview with Pierre Dupont, a Tourist Information Officer. In what order does he mention these points? Write 1–5.**

_____ **a** digital tourism

_____ **b** promoting tourism in Brussels

_____ **c** a service for business events

_____ **d** staff at the tourist office

_____ **e** writing promotional literature

4 **Match these words and phrases from the interview with the definitions.**

1 one-stop shop

2 face to face

3 seasonal event

4 newsletter

5 press release

a when you meet another person and talk to them

b official document giving information to the television, radio, etc.

c short report of news that is sent regularly to people

d single location offering several services

e something that is organized during a particular time of year

5 **Correct the errors in the comparative and superlative forms in these sentences. There is one incorrect word in each sentence.**

1 Fly-cruises to Antarctica are most expensive than boat cruises. _____

2 Antarctica is far from Australia than South America. _____

3 Greenland is not as cold that Siberia in winter. _____

4 Copper Canyon in Mexico is four times larger that the Grand Canyon. _____

5 The hurricane season is the worse time to visit the Bahamas. _____

6 Complete this article by putting the adjectives in brackets in the correct comparative or superlative forms. Use one or two words in each space.

Remote destinations

These are some of the world's most isolated locations. Adventurous travellers will come home ¹_____ (rich) in experience but poorer in pocket – the cost of visiting these places is much ²_____ (high) a more traditional holiday destination.

The tiny island of Rapa Nui (Easter Island) in the South Pacific has almost 900 gigantic stone statues (*moai*) carved by the island's ³_____ (early) inhabitants. Direct flights from Santiago, Chile travel 3,700 kilometres to island's airport, the ⁴_____ (remote) international airport in the world.

Antarctica is one of the ⁵_____ (unusual) places to visit in the world with its stunning landscapes, unique wildlife, and extreme climate, but it's not ⁶_____ (easy) of places to get to. The ⁷_____ (good) time to go is from November to March when temperatures can be as ⁸_____ (high) 4°C!

Kamchatka, a 1,250 km-long peninsula in the Russian Far East, is one of the world's ⁹_____ (beautiful) and wildest places. It is a region of glaciers, geysers and thermal springs with 300 volcanoes. 29 of them are still active. Kamchatka is also famous for its brown bears – some of ¹⁰_____ (large) bears in the world.

7 Read the article again and find the words and phrases that match their definitions (1–8). They are in this order in the text.

1 far from towns or other places where people live _____

2 not afraid of taking risks or trying new things _____

3 with less money _____

4 extremely small _____

5 extremely big _____

6 made by cutting wood or stone _____

7 extremely attractive or beautiful _____

8 being the only one of its kind _____

PRONUNCIATION

8)))) **3.2** Listen to six sentences. How many words can you hear? The contraction *It's* counts as one word. Listen again and complete the sentences.

1 It's_____

2 It's_____

3 It's_____

4 It's_____

5 It's_____

9)))) Listen again. <u>Underline</u> the stressed syllables in the sentences in Exercise 8, as in the example. Practise the pronunciation.

1 It's <u>cheap</u>er than <u>sum</u>mer.

1))) 3.3 **Read some questions (1–6) that visitors often ask in VICs, and match them to their answers (a–f). Then listen and write the numbers the tourist officer says.**

1 What time do the banks open? ____

2 Does the museum offer a group discount? ____

3 How long is the walking tour? ____

4 How much is the Museum Pass? ____

5 Do kids go free on public transport? ____

a From ____ a.m. to ____ p.m., Monday to Friday.

b For 2 days it's ____ euros and for 3 days it's ____ euros.

c It's approximately ____ km and takes about ____ .

d Yes, groups of ____ or more get ____ % off per person.

e Yes, children under ____ travel free, and ____ to ____ -year-olds pay child fares.

2))) 3.4 **Listen to a phone enquiry to a VIC in Galway, Ireland, and answer the questions.**

1 Why is the man calling?_____

2 What event is on in the town at the moment?_____

3 What does the tourist officer offer to do?_____

4 What is the man's name?_____

5 How is he travelling?_____

6 What does the tourist officer ask the man to do?_____

3))) **These phrases from the conversation are not exactly what Sháuna said. Listen again, if necessary, and change the phrases. Practise saying the phrases using polite intonation.**

1 Sháuna speaking. Can I help you?_____

2 When do you want the accommodation for?_____

3 Can I have your passport number, sir?_____

4 You need to phone the office in person to book the accommodation._____

5 I'll make the phone call for you._____

6 Would you like anything else?_____

4 Match the following visitors' questions (1–6) to the tourist officer's advice and recommendations (a–f).

1 Can you suggest a good place to eat?

2 Where can we do some shopping?

3 Could you recommend a place to stay?

4 What are the local attractions?

5 Where can we go for a day trip?

6 What's the best time to visit the city?

a The most popular option is a boat to the Aran islands, just off the coast.

b You might like to look at our accommodation list on the computer here.

c You could come in July for the Arts Festival or September for the Oyster Festival, our two main festivals.

d I'd recommend McDonagh's Seafood House if you like fish.

e It's well worth a visit to Lynch's Castle and the Spanish Arch.

f You should visit the Headford Road Shopping Centre. It has over 60 stores and free parking.

1 Read this news article. What is special about the town of Vulcan in Canada? Choose the correct option.

   a It is a small town where everyone loves science fiction.

   b It is the location of some famous television and film studios.

   c The town's name inspired it to become a tourist attraction.

Vulcan, Alberta

The tiny town of Vulcan, Alberta has a population of under 2,000. By coincidence, the town has the same name as the home planet of Mr Spock, a character in the popular TV and film series, *Star Trek*. This inspired the town to become a tourist attraction, and it is now the official *Star Trek* capital of Canada and a favourite destination for science-fiction fans.

Visitors to the town in western Canada can see the 800-piece *Star Trek* collection on display at the Vulcan Tourism & Trek Station – the tourist information office. They can also participate in The Vulcan Space Adventure virtual reality game and take a self-guided *Star Trek* Walking Tour of the town. The town's welcome sign is in English, Vulcan and Klingon!

2 Read the article again and find the words and phrases that match their definitions (1–4).

   1 people who have a strong interest in someone or something _____

   2 collection of objects or pictures shown in public _____

   3 images and sounds produced by a computer to represent a place or a situation _____

   4 not part of an organized group with a leader _____

3))) 3.5 Listen to two visitors giving feedback about their visit to Vulcan's tourist information centre. Tick (✓) the person who mentions the following.

	Visitor 1	Visitor 2
1 the *Star Trek* collection		
2 the souvenirs		
3 the local shops		
4 the virtual reality game		
5 the staff at the tourist office		

4))) Listen again and answer the questions.

   1 What does the first visitor like about the Trek Station? _____

   2 What is he not happy about? _____

   3 What does the second visitor like about the Trek Station? _____

   4 What can you wear at the Trek Station? _____

   5 How can the staff help you? _____

5 Match the two parts of the staff's suggestions for Vulcan's tourist service. Then put each suggestion into the correct category.

1 Let's offer a 5% ...	**a** organize an annual convention for Star Trek fans.	**Entertainment:** _____
2 We could ...	**b** we have a town festival and invite actors from the series?	**Gift shop:** _____
3 How about ...	**c** discount for visitors who spend over $50.	**Special events:** _____
4 Why don't ...	**d** showing Star Trek films in the station?	
5 Let's have trivia ...	**e** the website to sell our products to fans who can't visit us.	
6 We should use ...	**f** competitions that visitors and locals can participate in.	

4 PACKAGE TOURS

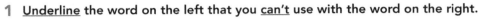

UNIT MENU

Grammar: past simple
Vocabulary: cultural heritage, packages, dates
Professional skills: city tours
Case study: design a package

1 <u>Underline</u> the word on the left that you <u>can't</u> use with the word on the right.

1 purpose-built / holiday / tourist / development	resort
2 package / transfer / city / all-inclusive	tour
3 fishing / charming / sandy / picturesque	village
4 tour / official / travel / tailored	guide
5 world heritage / art / historic / archaeological	site
6 architecture / religious / landmark / 19th century	building

2 Complete the spelling rules for regular verbs in the past simple.

1 If the verb ends in *e*, add ____ .

2 *y* changes to ____ before *-ed*.

3 *y* does <u>not</u> change if there is a ____ before it, e.g. *stayed*.

3 Complete the text on tourism development in Hawaii using the verbs in the box in the correct form.

> contribute   decrease   develop   die   discover   dominate   increase
> modernize   play   recover   try   visit

Hawaii is situated in Polynesia in the central Pacific Ocean and is made up of eight main islands. It became a state of the US in 1959. Because of its tropical climate, it is a popular all-year destination for tourists, surfers and scientists. The first Western visitor recorded was the British explorer Captain James Cook, who ¹_____ Hawaii, and ²_____ there on his final voyage to the islands.
19th century development in Hawaii ³_____ an important part in the increase of tourism which continued into the 21st century. Kilauea volcano was the islands' main attraction. In 1865, Hawaii's first hotel, Volcano House, was built at Halemaumau Crater for adventurous visitors. For 100 years sugar plantations ⁴_____ the economy until the workers went on strike and ⁵_____ to demand higher wages, which led to the end of the sugar industry.

With the end of sugar production, tourism ⁶_____ . When cars, hotels, and shopping malls arrived in Hawaii, they ⁷_____ the islands, and ⁸_____ to the growth of tourism. During the 20th century increasing numbers of tourists ⁹_____ Hawaii. The figure ¹⁰_____ to over 1 million in 1967.
Unfortunately, the native Hawaiian population ¹¹_____ . For this reason, some Hawaiians are very critical of tourism and its effect on their culture. Towards the end of the 2000s the number of tourists fell, but then ¹²_____ in 2011 because of an increase in arrivals from Canada, Australia, South Korea and China.

PRONUNCIATION

4))) **4.1** Listen to the pronunciation of the verbs from Exercise 3. Put them in the correct category according to the pronunciation of *-ed*, as in the examples.

/t/	/d/	/ɪd/
developed	continued	recorded

5 <u>Underline</u> the odd word in each group. Use a dictionary to help you. Give reasons for your answers.

1 mayor's house, shopping mall, parliament, town hall _____

2 art gallery, concert hall, national museum, pillar _____

3 palace, pyramid, residence, castle _____

4 roof, façade, building, window _____

5 tower, big wheel, bridge, classical _____

6 French, Medieval, Roman, Renaissance _____

6 Put the words in the questions about London's past in the correct order.

1 of Parliament / designed / the Houses / who _____

2 the first monarch / who / to live / was / in Buckingham Palace _____

3 Charles Dickens / the book, *Oliver Twist* / where / did / write _____

4 Shakespeare / did / his plays / where / produce _____

5 was renamed / London museum / which / Prince Albert / in memory of _____

6 Harrods, the famous / first open / when / department store / did _____

7 Match the questions (1–6) in Exercise 6 to the answers (a–f) below.

a The Victoria and Albert museum (the V&A). ____

b In 48 Doughty Street, now a museum. ____

c Queen Victoria. ____

d In 1849, when Henry Harrod opened a small shop. ____

e At the Globe theatre. ____

f The Victorian architect, Sir Charles Barry. ____

8 Complete the facts about London by using the verbs given to complete gaps 1–12. Use past simple, active or passive forms. You will complete gaps a–j in exercise 9.

Did you know ...?

• The Iceni tribe, led by the legendary Queen Boadicea, [1] _____ (destroy) the Roman city of Londinium nearly [a] _____ years ago, although it [2] _____ (rebuild) by the Romans.

• Most of the crown jewels in The Tower of London date from [b] _____ when new ones [3] _____ (make) for King Charles II and when they were first [4] _____ to the public. (show)

• Rat catchers and other pest controllers [5] _____ (can not) prevent epidemics of the plague. The Plague of 1664–5 [6] _____ (kill) over [c] _____ Londoners.

• The City is the business centre of London. England's famous architect, Christopher Wren, [7] _____ (design) many of its buildings in the [d] _____ century after the Great Fire.

• King George II [8] _____ (give) number 10 Downing Street to Sir Robert Walpole in [e] _____ . It then [9] _____ (become) the official residence of the British Prime Minister.

• In the detective stories of Sir Arthur Conan Doyle, Sherlock Holmes [10] _____ (live) at [f] _____ Baker Street. But the building that is the Sherlock Holmes museum is in fact number [g] _____ .

• The Houses of Parliament [11] _____ (complete) in [h] _____ but the original palace dates back to 1042. Big Ben is not the name of its world famous clock, but its [i] _____ -tonne bell.

• The London Eye is a 135-metre high observation wheel which [12] _____ (put up) to celebrate the millennium. On a clear day visitors have a [j] _____ -kilometre view of the capital in all directions.

9))) 4.2 Listen and complete gaps a–j in Exercise 8 with the correct number, figure or date.

4

PROFESSIONAL SKILLS

1 Match the tourists' questions (1–6) about two tours in England to the tour guide's answers (a–f).

1 Excuse me, who built the original baths?

2 Is it OK if I take a few photos of the staircase?

3 What's the 'neo-classical' style?

4 How far is it on the train from London?

5 Did you say lunch wasn't included?

6 Could you drop us off at our hotel?

a Yes sure, but please don't use a flash.

b The Romans.

c It's just under two hours on the train.

d That's right, but I can recommend a good café.

e Yes, of course, it's included in the tour price.

f It was the type of architecture from the early 19th century.

2 Match the tourists' questions (1–6) to the two tours in England, Bath spa (BS), or Harry Potter (HP).

1 _____ 2 _____ 3 _____ 4 _____ 5 _____ 6 _____

Bath spa tour
~~~~~~~~ ~~~~~~~~~~

This 8-hour tour includes the Roman Baths Museum, and an optional 2-hour spa.

The Romans created a complex of baths around the natural hot springs in Aquae Sulis, the Roman name for Bath. The modern Bath Spa opened in 2006 and has a rooftop pool.

Visit Bath's elegant streets.

1 hr 45 mins by train from London.

Price: £99.00 pp (train, entrance fee, spa session & lunch incl.)
~~~~~~~~~

Harry Potter tour

This one-day tour includes locations of the Harry Potter films in London and Oxford.

In London, visit the train station and platform 9¾.

In Oxford, see the grand staircase and the Great Hall that was the model for Hogwarts' Dining Hall.

Prices: 2–6 people: £590; minibus (7–11 people): £935.

Included: tour guide, pick up and drop off at your London hotel (entrance & meals not incl.)

3))) 4.3 Write the visitors' questions for the tour guide's answers. Then listen to the Harry Potter tour and check your answers.

1 Q: _____

A: Of course, a visit to platform 9¾ in King's Cross station is included.

2 Q: _____

A: No, I'm afraid entrance tickets and meals are not included in the tour.

3 Q: _____

A: We have one hour for lunch, from 1 to 2 p.m.

4 Q: _____

A: There's a shop that sells souvenirs over there next to the music store.

5 Q: _____

A: I said you can buy souvenirs in the shop over there.

1 Read the Transylvania tour information and complete gaps 1–5 with these headings. You will complete gaps a–h in Exercise 4.

> Duration   Not included   Price   Tour description   Tour itinerary

Central European Tours

Transylvania Tour

1_____

The picturesque region of the Carpathian mountains in Romania was the setting for many vampire movies and the inspiration for Bram Stoker's novel. This one-day tour takes you to Peles Castle ᵃ _____ , and Bran Castle – 'Dracula's' castle. The tour includes our ᵇ _____ tour guide, a typical Romanian lunch, and a visit to ᶜ _____ Brasov. Discover ᵈ _____ Vlad Tepes, who ruled Romania in the 15th century.

2_____ approx. 12 hr

3_____

Bucharest – Sinaia mountain resort, visit Sinaia monastery and Peles castle
Sinaia – Bran, visit Bran (Dracula's) castle, lunch
Bran – Brasov, walk in the old town and visit the City Hall
Brasov – Bucharest

4_____

ᵉ _____
2–3 persons: €110 pp
4–8 persons: €80 pp
Included
English-speaking driver / guide
Transport by car / minibus

5_____

Entrance fees (€11 pp)
ᶠ _____
Longer tours arranged on request
Why not take our ᵍ _____ 'vampire' tour ʰ _____ !

2))) 4.4   Listen to the tour in Bran castle and say if the sentences are true (T) or false (F).

1 Bran castle is mostly famous because of its charming views.   T / F

2 The castle dates back to the late 14th century.   T / F

3 It's easy to get lost in the castle.   T / F

4 It's very light because there are a lot of windows.   T / F

5 The man in the painting looks like one of the visitors.   T / F

6 Legend says that the heart of Queen Mary was kept in a silver box.   T / F

3)))   Complete the sentences with these prepositions. Listen again and check your answers.

> in   in   in   of   for   for   for   to

1 The castle is famous _____ its charm.

2 The castle dates back _____ 1377.

3 Its walls are made _____ stone.

4 We try to maintain the old traditions _____ Transylvania.

5 But did you know that _____ 1920 ...?

6 The legend says her heart was kept _____ this silver box.

7 Sit down _____ a moment.

8 I think it's time _____ lunch.

4 Improve the tour information in Exercise 1. Add the extra information (1–8) to the gaps (a–h).

1 Lunch (€14 pp)

2 local specialist

3 and celebrate Hallowe'en in a medieval castle

4 1 person: €160 pp

5 with its 160 rooms

6 the terrible legends of the real 'Dracula'

7 four-day

8 the medieval city of

5 HOTELS

UNIT MENU

Grammar: modal verbs
Vocabulary: hotel services and facilities, hotel trends, hotel charges
Professional skills: dealing with complaints
Case study: make a good hotel great

1))) 5.1 **Listen to a guest checking into a hotel and put the receptionist's actions into the order you hear them. The first item is given.**

_____ **a** Ask for the guest's passport or photo ID.

_____ **b** Tell the guest the breakfast times.

_1_ **c** Smile and greet the guest.

_____ **d** Ask if the guest needs assistance with luggage.

_____ **e** Give the guest the keycard and directions to the room.

_____ **f** Ask the guest for a credit card.

_____ **g** Wish the guest an enjoyable stay.

_____ **h** Confirm the reservation details.

2))) **Listen again and answer the questions.**

1 Why is the guest staying at the hotel?_____

2 What type of bed does she want?_____

3 When does the hotel charge the guest's credit card?_____

4 Where is the guest's room?_____

5 What time is breakfast?_____

6 Where is breakfast served?_____

3 **Complete what the receptionist says in Exercise 1. Use between one and three words. Check your answers in the audioscript on page 48.**

1 _____ see your passport or Photo ID, please?

2 _____ check that.

3 The _____ is included in your room rate.

4 _____ have your credit card, please?

5 _____ here, please.

6 _____ your keycard and room number.

7 _____ like the porter to take your luggage?

8 _____ and the convention.

4))) 5.2 **There are many 'silent letter' words in English with letters that are not pronounced. What are the silent letters in these words? Listen and check.**

1 buffet _____   **4** half _____   **7** would _____

2 could _____   **5** night _____

3 guest _____   **6** sign _____

5))) 5.3 **Put the second sentence in the correct order to make the first sentence sound more polite. Listen and check your answers.**

1 Let me see your reservation.

your / see / please / I / can / reservation

_____ ?

2 Give me your credit card.

have / credit card / may / your / I

_____ ?

3 Sign here.

you / here / sign / could

_____ ?

4 Do you want breakfast?

in the morning / like / breakfast / you / would

_____ ?

5 Do / you / want / the / porter?

I / the / call / for you / porter / shall

_____ ?

6))) **Look at the example. How does the speaker use intonation to sound more polite? Practise the intonation of the sentences in Exercise 5. Then listen again and check.**

↗   ↗

1 Can I see your reservation, please?

7 Match the words we commonly use together. Match 1–4 with a–d and 5–8 with e–h. Which are room facilities and which are hotel services and facilities?

1	walk-in	**a**	centre	**5**	in-room	**e**	pool	
2	baby	**b**	desk	**6**	ironing	**f**	safe	
3	fitness	**c**	cot	**7**	swimming	**g**	service	
4	front	**d**	shower	**8**	laundry	**h**	board	

Hotel services and facilities: _____   Room facilities: _____

8 Complete these sentences with six of the expressions from Exercise 7.

1 Guests can programme the _____ to open with a personal four-digit code.

2 You can phone our 24-hour _____ on 100 if you need anything.

3 Our _____ can collect your washing and ironing and return it the next day.

4 For families with infants, the hotel provides a _____ on request.

5 Baths are disappearing from many hotel rooms as guests prefer a spacious _____ .

6 The indoor heated _____ is 25 m long and 1.60 m deep and is open all year.

9 <u>Underline</u> the word in each group that <u>can't</u> be used with the noun on the right.

1 single, walk-in, double, king-size   bed

2 standard, twin, family, queen   room

3 executive, familiar, junior, luxury   suite

4 indoor, wi-fi, outdoor, heated   swimming pool

5 free, valet, secure, in-room   parking

6 half, breakfast, full, ironing   board

10 Put the words in the box into the correct category.

> ~~blanket~~ computer duvet fax mattress photocopier pillow printer
> sheet scanner shampoo shower gel soap toiletries towel

bed	bathroom	business centre
blanket		

11 Match the accommodation type in the box to the correct description.

> boutique   budget   business   hostel   luxury   resort

1 _____ : an inexpensive place where travellers, especially young people, can stay, often in dormitories.

2 _____ hotel: provides rooms for meetings, conferences and banquets. It has office services, as well as hi-tech rooms and leisure facilities.

3 _____ , or designer, hotel: offers chic accommodation with a high level of comfort and service.

4 _____ hotel: provides cheap accommodation in basic room with limited hotel facilities.

5 _____ hotel: usually in a popular holiday destination. It offers services and facilities for people on vacation, such as an entertainments programme.

6 _____ hotel: offers very high quality, full-service facilities to guests, such as 24-hour room service.

12))) 5.4 Listen to four people talking about their accommodation needs. Which type of accommodation in Exercise 11 is best for each person?

Guest 1: _____   Guest 2: _____   Guest 3: _____   Guest 4: _____

1 Use a prefix (*in, im, dis, un*) to form the opposites of these adjectives that we sometimes use to praise or complain about something.

1 _____ comfortable

2 _____ efficient

3 _____ experienced

4 _____ friendly

5 _____ happy

6 _____ helpful

7 _____ organized

8 _____ polite

2 Match the opposite adjectives.

1 affordable   **a** dirty

2 clean   **b** expensive

3 disappointing   **c** noisy

4 fast   **d** wonderful

5 polite   **e** rude

6 quiet   **f** slow

PRONUNCIATION

3))) 5.5 Many words in English have long vowel sounds. These are <u>underlined</u> in 1–5 below. Choose the word in each group that has a different vowel sound. Listen and check your answers.

1 /ɑː/ (card): p<u>a</u>rking, st<u>a</u>ff, f<u>a</u>st, sh<u>a</u>bby

2 /ɜː/ (sir): d<u>i</u>rty, p<u>i</u>llow, s<u>u</u>rname, f<u>u</u>rniture

3 /iː/ (please): cl<u>ea</u>n, w<u>ea</u>ther, d<u>ea</u>l, sl<u>ee</u>p

4 /ɔː/ (for): n<u>oi</u>sy, t<u>a</u>lk, b<u>oa</u>rd, fl<u>oo</u>r

5 /uː/ (room): v<u>ie</u>w, p<u>oo</u>l, r<u>u</u>de, t<u>o</u>wel

4))) 5.6 Listen to a guest complaining and choose the correct option.

1 The guest is in room ...

  a 306

  b 316

  c 360

2 What is he unhappy about?

  a the disappointing view

  b the noise from inside the hotel

  c the noise from outside the hotel

3 Why was the room noisy?

  a The window wasn't closed.

  b The air-conditioning was old.

  c It was at the back of the hotel.

4 The receptionist ...

  a is very helpful and friendly.

  b doesn't apologize for the problem.

  c offers an unsatisfactory solution.

5 In the end, the guest ...

  a decides to use the air-conditioning.

  b accepts the offer of an electric fan.

  c wants to move to another room.

5 Complete this response to the hotel guest's complaint in Exercise 4 with the correct preposition (*about, at, for, on, to, with*).

From:	info@continental.com
To:	talbot@tmail.us

Dear Mr Talbot

Thank you ¹_____ your email about your recent experience ²_____ our hotel. We welcome feedback from our guests.

I am sorry that your room was noisy and hot. I can understand that it is difficult to sleep over the sound of the sea. I talked to the reception manager ³_____ your complaint and she tells me that you requested a room ⁴_____ a sea view and you didn't close the window ⁵_____ night nor use the air-conditioning.

The reception staff offered to move you ⁶_____ a room ⁷_____ the back of the hotel at the time, which you refused. They also put a fan in your room.

I am also sorry to hear that you feel the member of staff who dealt ⁸_____ your complaint was unhelpful. It is not representative of our team who usually receive good feedback from guests. We try our best ⁹_____ all our guests and I'm sorry that we didn't meet your expectations ¹⁰_____ this occasion.

Once again, I apologize for the inconvenience caused during your stay with us. I hope you will come back soon and give us an opportunity to restore your confidence in our hotel.

1 **Look at the guest feedback questionnaire from The Safari Resort Hotel. Write the comments (a–f) in the correct place to continue what the guest wrote in the questionnaire (1–6).**

a The bathroom wasn't very clean and I had wet towels for a week.

b We waited for an hour for the bus to arrive because we were told the wrong time.

c They never said 'good morning' or smiled. One porter told me he was too busy to help me.

d He didn't even know the names of some of the animals!

e I waited 45 minutes for a sandwich. When it came, it wasn't what I ordered.

f The net around the bed had a big hole in it. I couldn't sleep all night!

The Safari Resort Hotel

	Good	Average	Poor
Reception			
Check-in and check-out	☒	☐	☐
Concierge services	☐	☐	☒
Bellboy services	☐	☐	☒
Courtesy of staff	☐	☐	☒

1 Staff were generally unfriendly and sometimes rude. _____

2 The concierge didn't give us the right details for the excursions. _____

Room			
Comfort	☐	☐	☒
Equipment	☐	☒	☐
Cleanliness	☐	☐	☒
Maintenance	☐	☒	☐
Room service	☐	☐	☒

3 The room was infested with mosquitoes. _____

4 The housekeepers were inefficient. _____

5 Room service was extremely slow. _____

Excursions			
Quality	☐	☐	☒
Guides	☐	☐	☒

6 The safari was overpriced. The jeeps are new but there is no guide. The driver only knew basic information. _____

2 **))) 5.7** **Listen to staff at the Safari Resort Hotel talking to the manager about the guest's feedback. Who is speaking?**

the concierge   the excursion driver
the housekeeper   the reception manager
the room service waiter

Speaker 1_____

Speaker 2_____

Speaker 3_____

Speaker 4_____

Speaker 5_____

3 **What does the manager need to do to improve the guest experience? Match 1–6 and a–f.**

1 Hire   a the excursions brochure.

2 Order   b the delays in room service.

3 Update   c an experienced nature guide.

4 Train   d an email apologizing to the guest.

5 Reduce   e staff in better customer service skills.

6 Write   f new mosquito nets and cleaning products.

UNIT MENU

Grammar: countable and uncountable nouns
Vocabulary: food and drink, food orders, catering
Professional skills: meeting customers' needs
Case study: rescue a restaurant

1 Put the words into four food groups.

apple	banana	~~beef~~	cabbage
carp	carrot	chicken	cod
cucumber	duck	lamb	mango
onion	orange	pineapple	potato
rabbit	salmon	trout	tuna

Meat	Fish
beef	
Fruit	**Vegetable**

2 A good dictionary has a lot of information about a word. Look at this extract from the Longman Dictionary of Contemporary English and label the parts a–f.

a definition

b indicates stressed syllable

c example sentence

d part of speech (noun, verb, adjective, etc.)

e countable or uncountable noun, or both

f symbol for American English alternative

1 _____ 2 _____ 3 _____ 4 _____

des.sert /dɪˈzɜːt/ $-ɜːrt/ n [C,U] sweet food served after the main part of the meal: **for dessert** *What are we having for dessert?*

5 _____ 6 _____

LONGMAN
Dictionary of
Contemporary
English
THE LIVING DICTIONARY
NEW

PRONUNCIATION

3))) **6.1** Put the other words from Exercise 1 into the correct group according to the stress pattern. Listen and check your answers. Which words have 'silent' letters?

O	Oo	Ooo	oOo
beef	apple		

4 Match the group of words to the categories in the box. Which word in each group is different and why? Put the word with the correct category.

beverages   condiments   dairy products
grain products   herbs and spices
seafood and shellfish

1 butter, cereal, cheese, milk, yoghurt _____

2 bread, mint, noodles, pasta, rice _____

3 decaf coffee, juice, milk, sparkling water, squid _____

4 clam, mussel, prawn, octopus, tea _____

5 curry, garlic, ketchup, paprika, parsley _____

6 ice cream, olive oil, pepper, salt, vinegar _____

5 Write the plural forms of the words in the table in the correct categories, as in the example.

~~anniversary~~   business   chef   customer
glass   guest   knife   lunch   man   mango
meal   order   potato   vegetable   waitress
woman

-s	-es	-ies	other
		anniversaries	

6 Read this advertisement for a catering company and choose the correct plural or singular form of the words in the box to complete it.

> allergy   child   company   dish   party   person   sandwich   tomato

Are you planning a ¹_____ for your child's next birthday?
Our ²_____ can help you with the food so you can relax
and enjoy the day. We specialize in catering for ³_____ and
young ⁴_____ . Our menu options include everything from
traditional ⁵_____ and cakes, to more healthy options, such as
⁶_____ , cheese and fruit. Snack food and buffets are popular
with kids, so we present party food on separate serving ⁷_____
and they can choose what they want. We also cater for special needs,
such as vegetarian diets and children with food ⁸_____ .

7)))) 6.2   Complete this restaurant dialogue with *some, any, much, many* or *lots*. Then listen and check.

Waiter: Would you like ¹ _____ drinks before you order your meal?

Sarah: Yes please. I'll have a sparkling water with ² _____ ice.

David: A tonic water for me, please. I don't want ³ _____ ice.

Waiter: Certainly, I'll get your drinks.

Sarah: There aren't ⁴ _____ customers in here.

David: It's still early. I expect there'll be ⁵ _____ of people later.

Sarah: And there aren't ⁶ _____ meat dishes on the menu.

David: It's a seafood restaurant Sarah! There are ⁷ _____ of fish dishes.

Sarah: Well, we haven't got ⁸ _____ time. Let's order when the waiter comes back.

David: Good idea. Fresh cod sounds good!

8 Use the clues to complete the crossword.

Across →

3 when you ____ a table you put plates, forks, etc. on it

5 a customer asks for this at the end of a meal

8 the ____ are dishes a restaurant is promoting

9 you eat with a ____ and fork

10 reservation

12 sweet food served after the main part of the meal

14 number of customers who are served during a shift

Down ↓

1 man who serves tables in a restaurant

2 container for drinks

3 a server's ____ is the group of tables he/she is responsible for

4 extra money customers give for good service

6 forks and spoons are examples

7 serviette

11 an ____ is the food and drink requested by a customer

13 when you ____ out of something you have no more of it

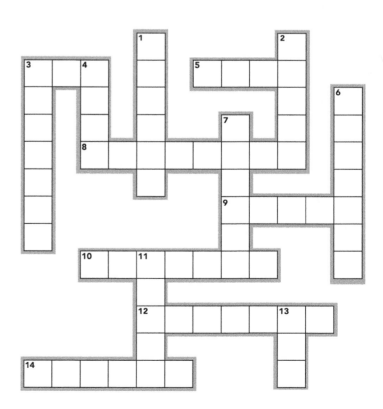

1 Complete the description of the three international dishes using the words in the box.

> added   Hungary   Iraqi   Korea   made   made of   marinated
> seasoned   served with   side dish   spicy   sprinkled

Goulash is originally from
1 _____ , a tasty
stew or a soup, usually
2 _____ with beef,
onions, vegetables, and
3 _____ with paprika
and other spices. Potato and
noodles (*galuska* in Hungarian)
are also 4 _____ in
some recipes.

Masgouf, or Masgûf, is a
traditional 5 _____
dish. Open-cut fish is
6 _____ in olive
oil, salt, pepper and tamarind,
and then barbecued. When
cooked, it is 7 _____
with lemon or lime juice
and 8 _____ rice,
flatbreads and salad.

Kimchi is a traditional
9 _____ vegetable
dish in 10 _____.
It's usually 11 _____
cabbage. Kimchi is a typical
12 _____ with most
meals, and also a common
ingredient in soups, stews and
rice dishes.

2))) 6.3   Listen to some diners ordering in a restaurant in Spain. Complete the description of the dishes. What do they order?

Pulpo a la Gallega
Boiled 1 _____ sprinkled
with paprika, 2 _____ and
3 _____.

Gambas Ajillo
4 _____/shrimp cooked in
olive oil with 5 _____ and
6 _____.

Verduras a la parrilla
7 _____ mixed vegetables:
8 _____/eggplant,
9 _____/zucchini, red peppers
and mushrooms.

Paella Marinera
10 _____ paella made with
rice, prawns, 11 _____,
12 _____, squid and sea bass.

The woman orders _____ for her starter.

The man orders _____ for his starter.

They order _____ for the main course.

3 Listen again and tick (✓) what the waiter said. Put a cross (✗) beside the phrase that is <u>not</u> appropriate in each group.

1
  a I'm sorry, I won't be a moment. _____
  b I'm very busy. Wait a moment. _____
  c I'll be with you in just a moment. _____

2
  a Sorry to keep you waiting. Are you ready to order? _____
  b Sorry about the delay. Would you like to order now? _____
  c Sorry I'm late. What do you want? _____

3
  a No, the chef can't change it. _____
  b I'll make a note for the chef. _____
  c I'll let the chef know. _____

4
  a Would you like some more bread? _____
  b Can I get you some more bread? _____
  c Here's some bread, do you want it? _____

4))) 6.4   Listen and write the phrases you hear. Who said each phrase, the waiter (W) or the diner (D)? Practise the pronunciation.

1 _____ W / D
2 _____ W / D
3 _____ W / D
4 _____ W / D
5 _____ W / D
6 _____ W / D

1 **Read this restaurant review and answer the questions.**

   1 What type of cuisine does Sakura serve? _____

   2 How many people can sit around the *hibachi*? _____

   3 Which two special diets does Sakura cater for? _____

   4 What will entertain children?_____

   5 Who will especially enjoy this restaurant? _____

   6 What's the best day and time to go with young children? Why?_____

Sakura

average price: €40 per head
set menu: €29

> **Checklist**
> ✓ vegetarian-friendly
> ✓ wheelchair access & disabled toilets
> ✓ private dining room (maximum 12 people)
> ✓ child-friendly
> ✓ highchairs available
> ✓ low-calorie dishes

Freshly cooked food and the theatrical performances of the chefs make this establishment very entertaining. Watch the chefs chop, throw around and chargrill your meat, fish and vegetables. Take your kids to see this spectacle.

The menu is mainly Japanese multi-course teppan-yaki style meals. Diners sit around a communal hot-plate (hibachi) table for eight. Each table's personal chef brings in the ingredients and prepares the food before your eyes. He then serves it, freshly cooked and steaming hot.

Prices aren't cheap but then meals such as the tuna steak served with teriyaki sauce, and the Sakura Delight, which is hibachi fillet steak with mushrooms, offer good value for money. And all the meals come with a prawn appetizer, a light onion soup and steamed rice.

The clientele consists of mainly families and noisy parties. On Sunday lunchtimes under tens get their own menu which includes a selection from chicken, burgers and pasta meals.

2 **Read the review again and find a word, part of a word, or phrase which means ...**

   1 suitable for particular people _____

   2 chairs with long legs, and a small table, for a baby or a small child _____

   3 meal with several parts _____

   4 people eating in a restaurant _____

   5 the price you pay is reasonable _____

   6 small amount of food eaten before a meal _____

   7 people who regularly use a shop or restaurant _____

   8 groups of people eating together in a restaurant _____

3))) **6.5** **Listen to five diners talking about their experience at Sakura. What does Sakura need to improve? Which diner comments on ...**

   1 food?   Diner ____

   2 entertainment?   Diner ____

   3 value?   Diner ____

   4 service?   Diner ____

   5 atmosphere?   Diner ____

4))) **6.6** **Listen to the owner and the front-of-house manager discussing possible solutions. Complete the sentences with <u>one to four</u> words.**

   1 Include some more free food, such as _____ and _____ .

   2 Possibly reduce the _____ to _____ or eliminate it.

   3 Offer _____ of one on drinks before _____ .

   4 Check the _____ and _____ as more people arrive.

   5 Employ more _____ especially for Friday and Saturday _____ and Sunday lunch.

7 NATURE TOURISM

1 Complete the information about Brazil using two words, one from each box, in gaps 1–8.

> animal   Atlantic   fifth   lowest   major
> mountain   South   tropical

> America   forest   largest   Ocean   point
> ranges   rivers   species

Brazil's geographic diversity

Brazil is the ¹ _____ country in the world, after Russia, Canada, China and the United States. It has an estimated population of over 190 million. Brazil shares a border with every country in ² _____ except for Ecuador and Chile. The ³ _____ lies to the east and Brasilia is the capital.

Brazil's geographic diversity includes hills, mountains, plains and highlands. The southeastern region consists of ⁴ _____ that reach a height of up to 1,200 metres. The highest mountain peak in Brazil is the Pico da Neblina at 2,994 metres, and the ⁵ _____ is the Atlantic Ocean.

⁶ _____ in Brazil include the world's second longest river, the Amazon, and its major tributary, the Iguaçu, with the world-famous Iguaçu Falls. The Amazon rainforest in Brazil is the largest ⁷ _____ in the world. It is estimated there are about four million different plant and ⁸ _____ in Brazil including pumas, jaguars, crocodiles, anteaters and armadillos.

2))) 7.1 Listen to Tom and Alicia talking about Tom's plans for a tour of Brazil and order the different parts of his itinerary 1–4.

____ Visit the Amazon rainforest

____ Fly to Salvador de Bahia

____ Stay in Rio de Janeiro

____ See the Iguaçu Falls

3))) Read the questions, listen again and decide which option (a, b or c) is <u>not</u> used.

1 Alicia asks ...
   a How long are you going for?
   b When are you flying to Rio de Janeiro?
   c Are you flying to Rio de Janeiro?

2 Tom says ...
   a The travel rep will meet us at the airport.
   b We're staying in a hotel that's 200 m from the beach.
   c We're not going to play volleyball, go surfing or sunbathe.

3 Alicia says ...
   a I suppose you'll visit Sugarloaf mountain.
   b You'll love Copacabana beach!
   c Are you going to see the falls?

4 Tom says after Foz do Iguaçu ...
   a We're going to the Amazon rainforest.
   b We're not getting to the Amazon rainforest until day five.
   c We're flying to Manaus and staying in the Amazon for five days.

5 Tom says ....
   a the showers aren't very warm and that'll be a problem.
   b the showers aren't very warm but that won't be a problem.
   c After that we're flying on to Salvador de Bahia.

6 Alicia says ...
   a Are you going to stay there for six days?
   b Where are you going to stay in Salvador?
   c I'm sure you'll have a great time!

4 Place these geographical features in the correct column below.

> ~~bay~~ cliff coast desert lake reef plain
> river valley waterfall

Sea	Fresh water	Land
bay		

PRONUNCIATION

5))) 7.2 Listen to the words in Exercise 4 and <u>underline</u> the part of the word that is stressed, e.g. <u>de</u>sert.

6 Write the words from Exercise 4 in the table below according to the pronunciation of the stressed sounds.

/e/ get	/ɪ/ tip	/iː/ see	/æ/ cat	/ɔː/ tour	/eɪ/ may	/əʊ/ show

7 Complete a guest's review about the Malaysian Borneo. The first letters of each missing word are given.

The Borneo Rainforest

We went on a 10-day tour of Borneo for adventure lovers including Orangutan [1] sp_____ in the jungle. The Danum Valley Conservation Area in the northeast has dense [2] ra_____ where you can see *orangutans*, *clouded leopards* and 300 [3] sp_____ of birds. We also took a flight south to the Gunung Mulu national [4] pa_____ which has spectacular views of the [5] ju_____ with its winding rivers, high [6] cl_____ and caves. Deer Cave is one of the largest in the world and is home to thousands of *bats*.

If you prefer comfortable accommodation, the Borneo Rainforest Lodge at Lahad Datu in the Danum Valley is wonderful. We paid extra to stay in a deluxe room overlooking the river with amazing [7] sc_____ . We heard the *rhinoceros* every day, the *orangutans* calling in the morning and the birds feeding in the [8] tr_____ .

Our guide asked us when we arrived what we wanted to see. We said *orangutans*, *rhinoceros*, *monkeys*, and *deer* and we were lucky to see them all! We didn't see the *clouded leopard*, although our [9] na_____ guide made sure we saw something new every day.

All the staff were extremely friendly and after [10] tr_____ in the jungle they always gave us a refresher towel, or dry towels when it rained.

TIPS: I recommend going to the [11] po_____ at night to see the *flying frogs, snakes* and *tarantula*! There are lots of horrible *leeches* and *sandflies* so bring a very strong [12] in_____ repellent. You can buy protective leech socks at the lodge.

8 Put the eleven kinds of wildlife in *italics* in the text in the correct group in the table below. Use a dictionary if necessary.

Mammals	Insects and spiders	Reptiles and amphibians

1 Put the outdoor activities in the box in the correct category.

> ballooning   bird watching   bungee jumping   canoeing
> flightseeing   horse riding   mountain biking   scuba diving
> snorkelling   snow boarding   trekking   wildlife spotting

Water sports	Air activities	Mountain sports	Wildlife activities

2 Put the extracts (a–h) from a presentation on Norway in the correct order.

_____ **a** If you want to experience them for yourself, you can go on a Northern Lights cruise. This takes you on a cruise with *spectacular scenery* across the Arctic Circle.

_____ **b** *So, if you love trekking, or want to see the Northern Lights, come to Norway!*

_____ **c** You'll see some *amazing scenery* when you go trekking along the fjords in our national parks. It's best to go in summer when you can stay in basic accommodation, in huts.

_____ **d** *Thank you for your attention. I'll be happy to take any questions now.*

_____ **e** Hello everyone, I'm Stig Engström. *First, I'd like to talk to you about our wonderful national parks, and then I'm going to show you one of Norway's greatest natural wonders – the Northern Lights.*

_____ **f** The Northern lights are the best thing about the Arctic in winter. *As you can see,* the night sky lights up with spectacular green, blue or red lights.

_____ **g** But what about the winter in Norway? Well, we have temperatures of minus 20°C, so the spring is the best time for skiing and snowboarding. But *have you ever heard of the amazing Northern Lights?*

_____ **h** *Norway has 23 national parks* as well as six on the islands. People say that Norwegians were born with skis on their feet. But one of the best ways to experience Norway is to go trekking.

3 Read the presentation again in Exercise 2 and answer the questions.

1 Which three outdoor activities are mentioned? _____

2 How many Norwegian national parks are there in total? _____

3 What kind of accommodation do Norwegian national parks offer? _____

4 What is the average temperature in Norway in winter? _____

5 When is the best time to see the Northern Lights? _____

6 Where does the cruise take passengers? _____

4 Match the expressions in *italics* from Exercise 2 with these functions for giving presentations. Function 6 has two answers.

1 Introducing your talk ___e___
2 Asking the audience a question _____
3 Giving interesting facts or figures _____
4 Referring to visuals _____
5 Connecting with the audience's interests _____
6 Using interesting adjectives _____
7 Ending your talk _____

5))) 7.3 Listen to six extracts from the presentation. How many words do you hear in each sentence? (5–9 words) Contractions count as one word e.g. *It's*. Write the sentence and then the number of words, as in the example.

> *It's best to go in summer.*   6 words

1 _____
2 _____
3 _____
4 _____
5 _____
6 _____

6))) Listen again and <u>underline</u> the stressed words in Exercise 5, as in the example.

It's <u>best</u> to <u>go</u> in <u>summer</u>.

1 Anila is preparing to give a presentation of a tour of Kerala, India at a tourism fair. Read her notes. Complete it with the expressions (a–h) to give more details and make it more interesting.

a As you can see from the itinerary,

b Did you know

c like elephants, deer and the great Indian tiger!

d Thank you for listening. Any questions?

e spectacular

f if you love wildlife and waterways, come to Kerala!

g its stunning scenery with

h Good evening everyone. I'm Anila Pillai from Wild Indian Tea Tours.

¹ _____ Today I'm going to tell you about our fantastic ten-day Kerala tour in India. ² _____ , first, you'll arrive in Kochi. Our tour representative will meet you at the train station and take you to your hotel. On day two, you'll go to Munnar to see ³ _____ its waterfalls and mountain goats. On day three, we'll transfer you to the Eravikulam National Park. You'll love the tea plantations there!

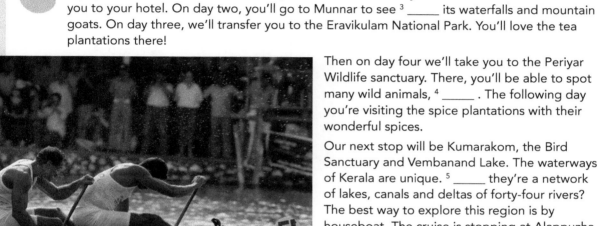

Then on day four we'll take you to the Periyar Wildlife sanctuary. There, you'll be able to spot many wild animals, ⁴ _____ . The following day you're visiting the spice plantations with their wonderful spices.

Our next stop will be Kumarakom, the Bird Sanctuary and Vembanand Lake. The waterways of Kerala are unique. ⁵ _____ they're a network of lakes, canals and deltas of forty-four rivers? The best way to explore this region is by houseboat. The cruise is stopping at Alappuzha, which is famous for its houseboats and exciting boat races.

Finally, you'll return to Kochi, where you're going to see a ⁶ _____ performance of Kathakali dance. So, ⁷ _____ OK, ⁸ _____ .

2)))) **7.4** Listen to some customers who went on the Kerala tour and choose the correct complaint (a or b) for each speaker.

Speaker 1

a The tour guide got lost in Kochi on the first day.

b They weren't met by the tour guide on their arrival.

Speaker 2

a They didn't see many wild animals.

b They didn't see the elephant sanctuary.

Speaker 3

a Parts of the tour were repetitive.

b They didn't visit the tea plantations.

Speaker 4

a The itinerary promised an event that they didn't see.

b They didn't enjoy the boat races in Alappuzha.

Speaker 5

a The guide took them dancing on the last night.

b The last day was tiring for some visitors.

3 Match the customer complaints (1–5) in Exercise 2 to Anila's suggestions (a–e) for improving the tour and making it more competitive.

a We could include more free time in the tour programme. ____

b How about making it clear that they probably won't see *all* the animals? ____

c We should give customers information on how to get to the hotel in case of emergencies. ____

d We shouldn't promise something that isn't going to happen during their visit. ____

e Why don't we offer the visit to the spice plantation as an optional extra? ____

8 AIR TRAVEL

UNIT MENU

Grammar: modal verbs
Vocabulary: airport facilities, giving directions
Professional skills: dealing with difficult passengers
Case study: the airport game

1 Match the two parts of the expressions to form places in an airport.

airport	control
baggage	desks
car	exchange
check-in	information
currency	park
duty-free	point
meeting	reclaim
passport	shops

2 Read the clues and complete the airport crossword.

Across →

1 place where your bags are checked for illegal goods when you go into a country
3 the _____ (Br Eng.) are also called the restrooms (Am Eng.)
8 a lift (Br Eng.) is also called an _____ (Am Eng.)
9 price you pay to travel somewhere by bus, train, taxi, plane, etc.
10 cases, bags, etc. carried by someone who is travelling
11 the place where you leave an airport building to get on a plane
12 you need a boarding _____ to take a plane

Down ↓

1 a _____ machine (Br Eng.) is also called an ATM (Am Eng.)
2 large basket on wheels that you use for carrying bags
4 another word for 10 across
5 place where an official person examines passengers and their possessions is a _____ checkpoint
6 the time when a plane leaves the ground and begins to fly is the _____ -off
7 place at an airport where people arrive when they get off a plane

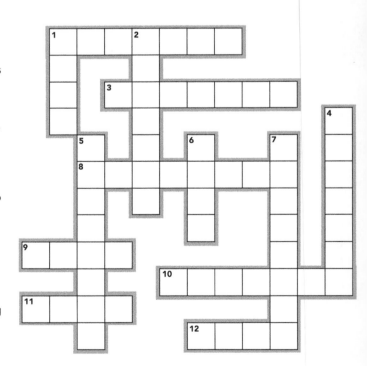

3))) 8.1 Listen to a conversation at Heathrow airport information desk in London. What does the passenger want to know?

_____

4))) The speakers in Exercise 3 use British English. The sentences below contain some American English words. Listen again and change anything you hear that is different. There are <u>ten</u> differences altogether.

1 Excuse me, can you tell me how to get to downtown London by public transportation? _____

2 Then take the subway from there to Victoria. _____

3 The fare is £19.00 one-way and £34 for a roundtrip ticket. _____

4 Just go straight on past the car rental offices and follow the signs. Then take the escalators or the elevator down to the lower ground floor. _____

5 It's about five minutes on the moving sidewalk. _____

6 No, you get that at the ticket booth or in the machines there. There are often long lines for the tickets. _____

5 Which sentence in each group (a, b or c) has a different meaning?

1 a Passengers must switch off all electronic devices.
b Passengers have to switch off all electronic devices.
c Passengers should switch off all electronic devices.

2 a Mobile phones shouldn't be used during the flight.
b Mobile phones can't be used during the flight.
c Mobile phones mustn't be used during the flight.

3 a Passengers should listen to the crew's instructions.
b Passengers are advised to listen to the crew's instructions.
c Passengers must listen to the crew's instructions.

4 a Large cases aren't allowed in the passenger cabin.
b You shouldn't bring large cases into the passenger cabin.
c You can't bring large cases into the passenger cabin.

5 a Passengers should label their luggage.
b It's a good idea for passengers to label their luggage.
c Passengers have to label their luggage.

6 a Passengers don't have to smoke on board.
b Passengers mustn't smoke on board.
c Passengers aren't allowed to smoke on board.

6 Complete the advice about staying healthy in the air with *should* or *shouldn't* and one of the verbs in the box.

> stretch   put   sit   ~~drink~~   have   pack

1 You <u>should drink</u> lots of water to stay hydrated.
2 You _____ in your seat for very long periods of time.
3 You _____ your legs and arms from time to time.
4 You _____ any essential medications in your hand baggage.
5 You _____ a heavy meal before you fly.
6 You _____ heavy bags into the overhead lockers.

7))) 8.2 Listen to some airport regulations and advice. Complete the sentences you hear with a maximum of <u>five</u> words.

1 Passengers _____ early.
2 You _____ security.
3 You _____ the trolleys.
4 Passengers _____ baggage.
5 You are only _____ carry-on bag.
6 Your passport _____ to the country.
7 Passengers _____ after clearing security control.

8 Which of the sentences in Exercise 7 express the following?

Advice _____
Prohibition _____
No obligation _____
Permission _____

PRONUNCIATION

9))) 8.3 Which do you hear *can* or *can't*? Tick (✓) the correct option.

	can	can't
1	_____	_____
2	_____	_____
3	_____	_____
4	_____	_____
5	_____	_____
6	_____	_____
7	_____	_____

1))) **8.4** **Listen to the conversation.**

1 Where are they in the airport? _____

2 What is the passenger's problem?
_____

2))) **Listen again and answer the questions.**

1 Which flight was the passenger on?
_____

2 When did it land? _____

3 What does the man ask for? _____

4 How does the passenger describe her baggage?
_____

5 What does the woman decide to do?
_____

3 **Complete the email of apology from an airline to another passenger. The first letters of each word are given.**

From:	chris.stewart@steadyair.co.uk
To:	msbertrand@bmail.com

Dear Ms Bertrand

On ¹ be_____ of Steady Air, I would like to ² ap_____ for the problems with your luggage on your recent flight with us from Glasgow to Madrid. I ³ un_____ how frustrating it is when you don't have your possessions.

Unfortunately, Glasgow Airport opened the new terminal on that day and, due to operational difficulties, a lot of luggage was lost, ⁴ del_____ or misdirected to other destinations.

I am sorry for any ⁵ in_____ this caused you. We can offer you compensation for your expenses on essential clothes and toiletries purchased before your luggage arrived. Please send your receipts to Customer Relations at the address on our website.

I am also ⁶ so_____ to hear that the staff at the lost luggage desk at the airport in Madrid were not very helpful. We are not directly responsible for the ground staff there but thank you for bringing this matter to our ⁷ at_____ .

I hope that you will fly with us again soon so that we can have an opportunity to restore your ⁸ co_____ in us.

Best regards

Chris Steward

Customer Relations

PRONUNCIATION

4))) **8.5** **Look at the examples and underline the word in each group that has a different sound from that in the example. Then listen and check. Place the odd word out in the correct group.**

1 /əʊ/ go	close, no, how, slow _____
2 /ɪə/ near	we're, here, date, year _____
3 /eɪ/ pay	wait, clear, plane, train _____
4 /ɔɪ/ toilet	right, noisy, coin, enjoy _____
5 /eə/ air	airport, fare, there, sign _____
6 /aɪ/ my	flight, licence , eight, aisle _____
7 /aʊ/ out	lounge, phone, hour, allowed _____
8 /ʊə/ tour	euro, sure, Europe, don't _____

5 *Homophones* **are words with the same pronunciation but with different meanings and spellings. Find the words in Exercise 4 that have the same pronunciation as the words below.**

1 fair _____
2 license _____
3 know _____
4 aloud _____
5 our _____
6 weight _____
7 plain _____
8 their _____
9 hear _____
10 I'll _____
11 write _____
12 ate _____

1))) **8.6** Listen to an interview with an airline purser. Complete what he says with a word or short phrase.

> The cabin crew have to be confident, friendly and [1]_____. You need to be [2]_____ but firm when dealing with difficult people. You have to stay [3]_____ under pressure and in emergencies. If a passenger is very rude or [4]_____ , keep your emotions and your [5]_____ under control. You also need to be [6]_____ towards people who are anxious or upset.
>
> I meet around [7]_____ people every day and difficult situations happen all the time. One of the most disturbing is when you discover that a passenger is [8]_____ . This is a serious danger for the passengers' [9]_____ and it is punishable by a fine. In this case, we have to [10]_____ and stop the passenger from leaving the aircraft until they arrive.

2 Flight attendants have to deal with many difficult situations. Match the situations (1–8) with the responses (a–h).

ON THE FLIGHT

1 During boarding a passenger has a suitcase that is too big for the overhead lockers.

2 After the cabin doors are closed, you see a passenger talking on her mobile phone.

3 While the cabin crew are giving the safety demonstration, two passengers are talking.

4 The same passenger as earlier is now texting on her mobile phone.

5 During the flight a very nervous-looking passenger jumps at every movement.

6 Several babies are crying persistently. A passenger complains about the noise.

7 Your nervous passenger is anxious about the change in the engine noises.

8 After landing, some passengers immediately start to open overhead lockers. Make an announcement.

a Could you switch off your mobile phone, please?

b Can we have your full attention for the next few minutes? Thank you.

c Rest assured we're just passing through some clouds.

d Please remain in your seats, with your seatbelt fastened until the captain has switched off the 'fasten seatbelts' sign.

e I expect it's because their ears are hurting. Would you like to listen to some music on our in-flight entertainment system?

f I can assure you that it's a perfectly normal sound, madam. Nothing to worry about.

g I'm sorry sir, that case is too big to take on board as hand baggage. We'll have to put it in the hold.

h I must insist that you switch it off now or you will not be allowed to take this flight.

9 HOTEL OPERATIONS

UNIT MENU

Grammar: present perfect simple
Vocabulary: housekeeping supplies, refurbishment, checking a hotel bill
Professional skills: checking out
Case study: choose a contractor

1 EHK Ray has a list of things to do. Complete the sentences using these verbs in the present perfect tense. Use contractions, e.g. *'s*.

> go   not inspect   check   not have
> not phone   not meet   speak   write

1 Ray _____ a list of things to do but he hasn't finished everything yet.

2 Ray's inspected floors one to three, but he hasn't _____ floors four to six yet.

3 He's supervised window cleaning but he _____ the garden yet.

4 He _____ to the laundry staff and has asked maintenance to repair a faulty washing machine.

5 Ray _____ with the hotel manager yet – but they've scheduled a meeting this morning for 11.00.

6 He _____ the linen supplier yet – he'll call later to order some new bed sheets.

7 He _____ lunch yet but he's taken a ten-minute coffee break.

8 Now, Ray _____ up to the fourth floor to supervise the new housekeeper.

2))) 9.1 Listen and write the questions for the answers you hear. There may be more than one possible question for each answer.

1 _____
2 _____
3 _____
4 _____
5 _____
6 _____
7 _____
8 _____

PRONUNCIATION

3))) 9.2 Put these regular verbs from Exercises 1 and 2 in the correct category according to the pronunciation of *-ed*. Listen, check your answers and practise saying them. When do we use the /ɪd/ ending?

> ask   check   clean   count   finish   inspect
> iron   phone   repair   supervise   talk   wash

/t/	/d/	/ɪd/

4 Complete the table with the equivalent word in American English.

American English	British English
1 _____	lift
2 _____	wardrobe
3 housekeeping _____	housekeeping trolley
4 taxi _____	taxi stand
5 _____	car park
6 _____	bill
7 _____	foyer
8 _____	toilet
9 _____	tap
10 _____	porter

5))) 9.3 Listen to an expert on hotel refurbishment and tick (✓) the best summary (A or B) of what he says.

A A simple refurbishment project takes about three months, but bigger projects can take six or seven. Coordination is the most important consideration, especially when remodelling public spaces. ____

B When running a hotel during refurbishment it is important to minimize disruption to guests, ensure their safety and coordinate the different contractors effectively. ____

6))) **Listen again and tick (✓) the points that the expert mentions.**

1 It's best if hotel refurbishment is done in three different phases or stages. ____

2 Guests rooms are bigger now than before. ____

3 Hotel management needs to have a good relationship with guests. ____

4 Contractors need to work at least six days a week during refurbishment. ____

5 Customers today want stylish hotels with modern suites and spas. ____

6 Complete remodelling can take more than 16 weeks. ____

7 The hotel has to coordinate the work carefully and make sure it's safe for guests. ____

8 Hoteliers should know the exact finishing date to minimize disruption. ____

7 **Match the words from the listening to the correct definitions. Look at the audioscript on page 50 to help you.**

> builder   close down   coordination   defect
> disruption   fittings   interior designer
> remodelling   operations   refurbishment

1 outside parts of a piece of equipment that makes it possible to use or handle _____

2 activity of decorating and repairing a building or hotel in order to improve its appearance _____

3 the organization of people or things so that they work together well _____

4 changing the complete shape, structure or appearance of a building _____

5 a person or a company that builds or repairs buildings _____

6 a person who designs the inside of a building _____

7 a fault or a lack of something that means that something is not perfect _____

8 a situation in which something is prevented from continuing in its usual way _____

9 the work or activities done by an organization, or the process of doing this work _____

10 stop being open to the public for a period of time _____

8 **Match the group of words to the categories in the box. Which word in each group is different? Why? Put the word with the correct category.**

> bed linen   cleaning products   fittings
> furniture   guest room items   refurbishment

1 pillowcase, sheet, bleach, mattress, blanket _____

2 polish, detergent, disinfectant, duvet, stain remover _____

3 toiletries, wardrobe, glasses, towel, pen _____

4 design, restoration, upgrade, stylish, chandelier _____

5 bed, bedside table, notepad, desk, armchair _____

6 sink, anti-theft hangers, hairdryer, remodel, mirror _____

PRONUNCIATION

9))) **9.4** **Put the words below in the correct group according to the word stress. Listen and check your answers.**

> ~~design~~   designer   extend   extension
> furniture   innovation   lobby
> refurbish   renovate   renovation
> restore   restoration   stylish

oO	Oo	oOo	Ooo	ooOo
design				

HOTEL OPERATIONS

1))) **9.5** **Put the check-out dialogue in the correct order (1–5). Then listen or read the audioscript on page 51 and check your answers.**

____ **Guest** No, thanks. Your colleague ordered one this morning.
Receptionist OK. We look forward to seeing you again. Bye!

____ **Guest** It's Fernando de la Cruz.
Receptionist Ah, yes. Here's your folio. You pre-paid one night, that's $174, so the balance due is $274. Could you enter your PIN here?

____ **Guest** Great. We loved the suite. But we couldn't use the spa on our first night because it was closed.
Receptionist I'm sorry to hear that. I'm afraid the spa closes at 9 p.m. Here's your receipt. Would you like me to order you a taxi?

____ **Guest** Hi, we'd like to check out, please.
Receptionist Good morning. May I have your name, please?

____ **Guest** Sure.
Receptionist How was your stay with us?

2))) **Complete the sentences (1–6) with what the receptionist said, using <u>three</u> words in each gap. Then match them with the correct function (a–f).**

1 Good morning. _____ _____ _____ your name, please?
2 _____ _____ _____ stay with us?
3 _____ _____ _____ hear that. I'm afraid the spa closes at 9 p.m.
4 _____ _____ _____ due is $274.
5 _____ _____ _____ me to order you a taxi?
6 _____ _____ _____ to seeing you again.

a offer help
b deal with any complaints
c greet the guest and ask for their nam
d say goodbye
e confirm the amount to pay
f enquire about their stay

3))) <u>Underline</u> **the words the receptionist stresses in the expressions in Exercise 2. Then listen again to check. Why are these words stressed? Practise saying the expressions.**

4 **While waiting for his taxi, Mr de la Cruz spots a mistake in their bill. What is it? Choose the correct option for the receptionist's reply.**

a I'm sorry about that, but the bill is correct, madam. Have a good trip!
b I do apologize about that. I'll print you a new bill and we'll pay back the difference of $100.
c I'm very sorry about that. You're right, the balance due is $374 dollars, not $274.
d Sorry, my mistake. The total amount is still the same but would you like a new bill for your records?

Hotel Carribean Spa

Invoice: 38872
Name of guest: Fernando de la Cruz
Room: 228

Dates	Description	Cost per night	Pre-paid	Amount
29th April – 1st May	2 nights, 2 adults FB May holiday promotion	$174.00	$174.00	$348.00

Total $348.00

Pre-paid $74.00

Balance due   <u>$274.00</u>

1 Read the newspaper stories. Match the sentence beginnings (1–4) with their endings (a–d) to make complete sentences.

1 This company has received
2 This company has been recognized
3 Staff at this company are happy because
4 The owner of this company has stolen items

a from hotels and their guests.
b they have good working conditions.
c an award for quality in hospitality.
d for its excellence in cleaning services.

2 Match each sentence from Exercise 1 with one of the stories A–C. Which story has two sentences?

A _____   B _____   C _____

BEST IN THE US

Clean & Sheen has won a Best US Business award for its cleaning services. The Boston firm was presented the award for its innovation and use of environmentally safe products. Company director, Melody Waters, who set up the company after working as an Executive Housekeeper, thanked her great team. Staff say they enjoy working for the firm because they get training, regular breaks and a fair wage.

New England hospitality

The Devonshire Sands hotel has received a Certificate of Excellence for its hospitality. 'The hotel has modernized the restaurant and spa without losing the hotel's New Hampshire feel', says hotel manager Emilio Mendez, who supervised its refurbishment. Emilio explains the key to its success. 'We're known for our elegant furnishings, modern facilities, and high standards of service.'

Cleaning couple clean out hotels

'The Cleaner', Tracy Mills, has been arrested for robberies at various hotels and motels in New Hampshire. Ms Mills, together with her brother Evan, convinced hoteliers to contract the services of Cleaning on Wheels. The couple obtained easy access to rooms, and stole from guests before escaping with housekeeping carts filled with cash, jewellery and other stolen hotel items.

3 Who do you think said these things: Emilio (E), Melody (M), or Tracy (T)?

1 'I set up my company after working for several years in housekeeping.' ____
2 'We're known for our elegant furnishings, luxury facilities, and high standards of service.' ____
3 'We only took a few towels and cash from bedside tables – we thought it was a gratuity.' ____
4 'I suspected them when I noticed that room items were missing. There were no guests that week.' ____
5 'I'd like to thank our fantastic team.' ____
6 'I've worked with Evan for years – he recommends my business to hotel managers.' ____

4))) 9.6 What can hotels do to avoid hotel theft? Tick (✓) the four best options. Listen to the hotel manager, Emilio, and check your answers.

1 Install security cameras in all guest rooms and public areas. ____
2 Contract more security staff. ____
3 Ask guests to go through a security check. ____
4 Declare an amnesty and ask past guests to return valuable items. ____
5 Contract private detectives. ____
6 Report suspicious guests to the police. ____

10 MARKETING

UNIT MENU

Grammar: first conditional

Vocabulary: marketing and promotions, tourism trends

Professional skills: negotiating

Case study: promote a region

1 Complete the South Korean tourism products (1–5) and market segments (a–e) with the correct options below. Then match the products to the market segments.

> adventure   city break   family   luxury   older   professional   retired
> student   three-star   working holiday

Tourism product

1 _____ in Seoul in a 5-star hotel

2 extreme sports _____ holiday

3 7-day package in a _____ hotel on Gyeongpo Beach

4 _____ 2-week Far East cruise

5 low-cost _____ on a social project

Market segment

a _____ with young children

b _____ couple (60–85)

c low-income _____ (19–24)

d young _____ (25–44)

e _____ professional (35–59)

2 Look at the definitions and complete the crossword with marketing words.

Across →

1 a company or person that pays for a show, broadcast, or sports event in exchange for the right to advertise at that event

5 a piece of paper with an advertisement on it, given to people in the street or pushed through a door

6 exchange information or talk with other people, using words, signs, or writing

7 an image, some words, or a short film, which persuades people to buy a product or use a service (abbreviated form)

9 a short phrase that is easy to remember and is used in advertisements, or by organizations

10 to supply goods to shops and companies so that they can sell them

Down ↓

2 help sell a new product, service, country, etc. by offering it at a reduced price, or by advertising it

3 business activity which involves collecting information about what things people buy and why they buy them

4 series of actions to achieve a particular result in politics or business, especially in marketing or advertising

8 aim to have an effect on a particular group or area

3 Complete the gaps in the article about online marketing (1–5) using the phrases (a–e).

a booking restaurants, activities, and transport during a trip

b destinations today are marketing themselves by themes

c already communicate directly with guests and customers

d has gone online

e taking part in social networks

Online tourism marketing

The tourism industry ¹ _____ . Digital marketing and promoting online bookings for package holidays will continue to be the main focus in tourism marketing in the near future. Hoteliers ² _____ using social media websites and social media will continue to play an important role.

Tourism marketing departments are spending more on online marketing and will also focus on Public Relations and tactical advertising, targeting specific groups of customers using online social networks and smartphones. Many travellers are using their mobile phones, from booking their trip to ³ _____ after their trip. More people have become 'social travellers', communicating via social media sites, and ⁴ _____ .

In addition, destinations are also modernizing their traditional marketing strategies. With the development of the internet, ⁵ _____ rather than by geographical location. Relaxation, discovery and enjoyment used to be the typical focus of travellers, but nowadays themes such as activities, health, and fun-learning are also becoming more popular.

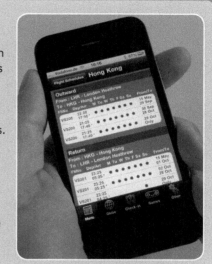

4 Complete the word formation table below. Use the text in Exercise 3 to help you.

Noun (thing)	Noun (person)	Verb
booking	–	¹ _____
² _____	developer	develop
discovery	³ _____	⁴ _____
⁵ _____	–	enjoy
learning	⁶ _____	learn
⁷ _____ / _____	marketeer	market
relaxation	–	⁸ _____
tourism	⁹ _____	¹⁰ _____
¹¹ _____	¹² _____	travel

5 Find and correct any errors in these conditional sentences about Chinese tourism. Not all sentences contain an error.

1 If more Chinese people travel abroad, China becomes a major player in world tourism. _____

2 If the number of Chinese tourists travelling outside Asia grows, countries like France and Germany will continue to be popular destinations. _____

3 If Asian economies will continue to do well, Asian consumers will get richer. _____

4 The Chinese will be welcome guests if they spend most of their travel budget on shopping. _____

5 Group tours are probably less popular than individual travel when Asian tourists become more demanding. _____

6 When Chinese tourists become less interested in sight-seeing, they won't spend more on entertainment and relaxation. _____

7 Travel companies won't have to translate their websites into Chinese when the Chinese travel market changes. _____

8 If more Chinese people go abroad, they'll probably want more services like slippers in guest rooms, Chinese menus and Chinese-speaking staff in museums. _____

1))) **10.1, 10.2, 10.3** Listen to some negotiations and match the situations (1–3) to the outcomes (a–f). Three of the outcomes are <u>not</u> used.

1 a shop assistant is persuading a customer to buy some clothes ____

2 two receptionists are talking about swapping (changing) shifts ____

3 a couple is negotiating the choice of menu for their wedding ____

a The customer buys two for the price of one.

b The customer buys three beach dresses.

c The manager will probably swap shifts with one of the receptionists.

d One of the receptionists will swap shifts with their colleague.

e If the couple choose menu 4, they'll reduce the guest list.

f If the couple choose menu 5, they'll reduce the guest list.

2 Match the expressions (1–8) with the correct negotiating tactics (a–d) below. Each of the tactics is used <u>twice</u>.

1 We have an offer today of two for the price of one. ____

2 And for only 65 TRY, I'll give you a third dress. ____

3 How does that sound? ____

4 They're great in hot weather, *and* they wash very well. ____

5 I'm sorry, but I can't do it this time. ____

6 When you ask me for a favour next time, I won't swap with you! ____

7 It's certainly more economical at £70 per person. ____

8 Would you like a moment together to discuss this? ____

a asking for a response

b offering a concession

c saying 'no'

d talking about the benefits of a product or service

PRONUNCIATION

3))) **10.4** Complete the sentences for talking about possibilities when negotiating. Use one to three words. Contractions count as <u>one</u> word. Listen and check your answers.

1 If you _____ (take) this lovely scarf, I _____ (give) you the lot for 75 TRY.

2 How much _____ (it/be) if I _____ (buy) another dress?

3 If you _____ (ask) Amanda nicely, perhaps she _____ (work) your shift next weekend.

4 I _____ (swap) with you the following weekend if that _____ (help).

5 If you _____ (not/invite) all your cousins, I _____ (agree) to a more expensive menu.

6 We _____ (be/able to) afford a better menu if your mother _____ (not/invite) all her friends.

7 How much _____ (it/cost) if we _____ (choose) menu 4 and have 110 guests?

8 If you _____ (decide) on menu 4 and 110 guests, it _____ (come) to £9,300.

4))) Underline the words that the speakers stress in the sentences in Exercise 3. Then listen again and check your answers. Practise saying the sentences.

1 **))) 10.5** Listen to some speakers talking about tourism marketing campaigns. Which cities or countries are they talking about? Write the destinations and then match the destinations (1–3) to the suggested slogans (a–c).

1 _____   a The bigger, the better!

2 _____   b Film, shopping and fun!

3 _____   c Magnificent – with love!

2 **)))** Listen again and complete what the speakers say about the destinations (1–9).

> My city is the centre of the Hindi film industry, known as ¹ _____. It's also a ² _____ paradise with exclusive boutiques, ³ _____ markets and mini-bazaars.

> This year our tourism ⁴ _____ wanted to create a new marketing campaign that shows our capital has ⁵ _____ , and a ⁶ _____ for visitors, too.

> It should highlight the idea of ⁷ _____, shopping, and ⁸ _____. ... it also needs to communicate the ⁹ _____ that we're a huge country.

3 Complete the ten tourism values using words from the box.

> beaches   beauty   culture   food   money   nightlife
> ~~people~~   resorts   weather   activities

1 adventure _____   6 natural _____

2 friendly   *people*   7 value for _____

3 delicious _____   8 exciting _____

4 history and _____   9 unspoilt _____

5 luxury _____   10 warm _____

4 Look at the profile of the fictional country of Hedonia. Which values from Exercise 3 could a marketing campaign focus on to develop its tourism industry? Choose **six** possible values.

Hedonia

- Capital city: Littletown
- Population: 40 million
- Main airport: 35 km from Littletown
- Economy: it is a fast-growing developing country with a young tourism industry
- Climate: partly continental and partly sub-tropical
- Geography: diverse with hills, rivers, lakes, rainforest, and beaches
- Main attractions: ancient ruins, unspoilt beaches, national parks, local festivals, simple and cheap food
- Points to develop: accommodation is basic; nightlife is quiet in Littletown; people are not very outgoing; the country needs new roads and another major airport; central Littletown is not very safe.

5 Complete the proposals by the National Tourist Board for promoting Hedonia abroad. Choose options a or b.

1 If we build a new airport near the sea, we'll be able to ...

   a develop large beach resorts.

   b promote sustainable tourism.

2 We'll be able to improve transport and communication if we ...

   a don't cut down forests.

   b build better roads.

3 But if we want to promote family holidays, we'll need ...

   a big resorts with budget hotels and attractions.

   b luxury resorts and small, boutique hotels.

4 We can keep our national parks if we offer ...

   a adventure activities and nature tours.

   b shopping and evening entertainment.

5 If we want to attract more solo travellers to the capital, we'll have to ...

   a promote our local festivals and historic sites.

   b implement better safety measures.

6 And we'll need more restaurants, cafés and cinemas if we want to ...

   a promote Hedonia as a top destination.

   b improve the nightlife in the capital.

6 Choose the best marketing slogan for promoting Littletown.

   a Littletown – If you've never been there, you'll never know, will you?

   b There's no town like Littletown.

   c Littletown – very friendly and safe!

TOURISM TERMS

People

ADL	Adult
CHD	Child
INF	Infant (up to two years old)
MR	Mister
MISS	used before a single woman's family name
MRS	used before a married woman's family name
MS	Used before a woman's family name when she does not want to be called 'Mrs' or 'Miss'
PAX	Passengers
VIP	Very important person
VFR	Visiting friends and relatives

International organizations

ETC	European Travel Commission
EU	European Union
IATA	International Air Transport Association – industry trade group for airlines which regulates international air travel
ICAO	International Civil Aviation Organization
IOC	International Olympic Committee
ISO	International Organization for Standardization
NTO	National Tourism Organization (organization a government uses to promote the country)
TIC	Tourist Information Centre
UN	United Nations
UNESCO	United Nations Educational, Scientific and Cultural Organization
VIC	Visitor Information Centre
WTO	World Tourism Organization (also UNWTO)
WHS	World Heritage Site

Jobs in tourism

ASST	Assistant
CEO	Chief Executive Officer
CFO	Chief Financial Officer
CV	Curriculum vitae
DOB	Date of birth
EHK	Executive Housekeeper
FOM	Front Office Manager
FT	Full-time
GM	General Manager
HK	Housekeeper
HQ	Headquarters
HR	Human Resources
MOD	Manager on Duty
PERM	Permanent position
PT	Part-time
TA	Travel agent
TEMP	Temporary position
P/H	Rate of pay per hour
P/W	Per week
P.A.	Per annum (annual salary)

Days

MON	Monday
TUE or TUES	Tuesday
WED	Wednesday
THU or THURS	Thursday
FRI	Friday
SAT	Saturday
SUN	Sunday
M–F	Monday to Friday

Months

JAN	January
FEB	February
MAR	March
APR	April
MAY	May
JUN	June
JUL	July
AUG	August
SEP or SEPT	September
OCT	October
NOV	November
DEC	December

Times and time zones

A.M.	from midnight to noon
P.M.	after noon

12-hour clock	24-hour clock
12:10 a.m.	0010
03:05 a.m.	0305
07.59 p.m.	1959

The 24-hour clock is simpler than the 12-hour clock. It uses four continuous digits (from 0000 to 2400) and there is no A.M. or P.M.

CST	Central Standard Time
EST	Eastern Standard Time
GMT	Greenwich Mean Time
PST	Pacific Standard Time
UTC	Coordinated Universal Time
WST	Western Standard Time
24/7	24 Hours a Day, 7 Days a Week
HRS	hours
WKS	weeks

Money and prices

ATM	Automatic teller machine (Am Eng), Cash machine (Br Eng)
EXCL	Exclusive (not everything is included in the price)
FIT	Fully inclusive tour
GIT	Group inclusive tour
GST	General sales tax (Am Eng)
IBAN	International bank account number
IIT	Individual inclusive tour
INCL	Inclusive
IT	Inclusive tour
PIN	Personal identification number
POS	Point-of-sales terminal (small hand-held computer for servers to take orders and calculate bills)
PP	per person
VAT	Value added tax (Br Eng)

Email and letters

ASAP	As soon as possible
BTW	By the way
FYI	For your information
CC	Carbon copy (when a copy of a letter is sent to more than one person)
ENC	Enclosure (when other papers are included with a letter)
PS	Postscript (when you want to add something after you've finished and signed it)
RSVP	Please reply

ISO Currency codes

* World's top ten most traded currencies

AUD   Australian Dollar*
CAD   Canadian Dollar*
CNY   Chinese Yuan Renminbi
EUR   Euro*
GBP   United Kingdom Pound*
HKD   Hong Kong Dollar*
INR   Indian Rupee
JPY   Japanese Yen*
KRW   South Korean Won
MXN   Mexican Peso
NOK   Norwegian Krone*
PLN   Polish Zloty
RUB   Russian Ruble
SEK   Swedish Krone*
CHF   Swiss Franc*
THB   Thai Baht
TRY   Turkish Lira
USD   United States dollar*

Hotels

AC   Air conditioning
AI or ALL INCL   All inclusive (price includes accommodation and all food, drink and activities)
BB   Bed & breakfast (price includes accommodation and breakfast only)
DBL   Double room
DLX   Deluxe room
FB   Full board (price includes accommodation and all meals)
HB   Half board (price includes accommodation, breakfast and evening meal)
HTL   Hotel
NTS   Nights
RO   Room only (price for accommodation only)
SC   Self-catering accommodation
SGL   Single room
STD   Standard room
TRPL   Triple room
TWN   Twin room
TWNB   Twin room with bath
TWNS   Twin room with shower
WC   Toilet
YHA   Youth Hostel Association

Air travel

ARR   Arrival
ATC   Air traffic control
DEP   Departure
ETA   Estimated time of arrival
ETD   Estimated time of departure
ID   Identification
LCC   Low-cost carrier
OW   One-way
RT   Return (Br Eng) Round trip (Am Eng)
SOP   Standard operating procedure
TRSF   Transfer

IATA codes

IATA codes are three-letter codes used for cities and airports in the travel industry. When a city has more than one airport it needs two types of code, a city code and a code for each airport.

LON   CITY CODE for London, UK
LCY   AIRPORT CODE for London City, London
LGW   AIRPORT CODE for Gatwick, London
LHR   AIRPORT CODE for Heathrow, London
LTN   AIRPORT CODE for Luton, London

World's busiest airports

(by international passenger traffic)

LHR   London Heathrow Airport, UK
DXB   Dubai International Airport, United Arab Emirates
HKG   Hong Kong International Airport, Hong Kong
CDG   Paris Charles de Gaulle Airport, France
SIN   Singapore Changi Airport, Singapore
FRA   Frankfurt Airport, Germany
AMS   Amsterdam Airport Schiphol, Netherlands
BKK   Suvarnabhumi Airport, Bangkok, Thailand
ICN   Incheon International Airport, Seoul, South Korea
NRT   Narita International Airport, Tokyo, Japan

Most visited cities in the world

PAR   Paris
LON   London
BKK   Bangkok
SIN   Singapore
KUL   Kuala Lumpur
NYC   New York
DXB   Dubai
IST   Istanbul
HKG   Hong Kong
SHA   Shanghai

ISO Country codes

ISO (International Organization for Standardization) is the most widely used international standard.

*The ISO two-letter country codes are used for internet domains with a few exceptions, most notably UK (not GB) is used for the United Kingdom's internet domain.

Country	ISO 2-letter code*	ISO 3-letter code
Australia	AU	AUS
Austria	AT	AUT
Bhutan	BT	BTN
Canada	CA	CAN
China	CN	CHN
Costa Rica	CR	CRI
France	FR	FRA
Germany	DE	DEU
India	IN	IND
Italy	IT	ITA
Kenya	KE	KEN
Korea, Republic of	KR	KOR
Malaysia	MY	MYS
Mexico	MX	MEX
New Zealand	NZ	NZL
Peru	PE	PER
Poland	PL	POL
Russia	RU	RUS
Spain	ES	ESP
Thailand	TH	THA
Turkey	TR	TUR
United Kingdom	GB/UK	GBR
United States	US	USA

AUDIO SCRIPT

Unit 1

1.1
Australia: Australian
Britain: British
China: Chinese
France: French
Germany: German
Italy: Italian
Spain: Spanish
USA: American

1.2
Brazil: Brazilian
Canada: Canadian
Greece: Greek
Ireland: Irish
India: Indian
Japan: Japanese
Kenya: Kenyan
Korea: Korean
Mexico: Mexican
Norway: Norwegian
Poland: Polish
Portugal: Portuguese
Russia: Russian
Thailand: Thai
The Netherlands: Dutch
Turkey: Turkish

1.3
A, H, J, K
B, C, D, E, G, P, T, V
F, L, M, N, S, X, Z
I, Y
O
Q, U, W
R

1.4
W = British woman, M = Japanese man
W Next please.
M Hello, I want two tickets to Manchester city centre.
W Leaving from London Euston?
M Yes.
W Single or return?
M Sorry. I don't …
W Do you want to travel one-way or return to London?
M Return, please.
W When do you want to travel?
M Tomorrow morning, and return to London on Sunday evening.
W So that's two return tickets from London Euston to Manchester Piccadilly. Leaving Friday 16th March and returning Sunday 18th March.
M Yes, that's right.
W OK, the cheapest fare is £80.20 return. Trains leave Euston at 9 a.m., 9.20 and 9.40. Would you like a later train?
M No, 9 o'clock is fine. What time does it arrive in Manchester?
W Journey time is two hours seven minutes, arriving at 11.07.
M And the return times? We'd like to leave Manchester about 6 o'clock.
W 6 a.m. or 6 p.m.?
M 6 in the evening.

W There are trains at 18.15, 18.35 and 18.55.
M What time does the 6.15 train arrive in London?
W At 8.27 in the evening.
M Yes, OK. That's good.
W So, that's £160.40 in total. How would you like to pay for that?
M By credit card …

1.5
W = British woman, M = Japanese man
W Old Trafford Booking Office.
M Oh, hello. When is the match this weekend?
W They're playing Arsenal this Saturday, 17th of March at 1.30.
M Oh good. I'd like two VIP tickets, please. How much is that?
W That's two hundred and ninety pounds per person, plus VAT.
M What's VAT?
W It's a 20% sales tax.
M Oh, I see.
W Can I have your name, please?
M Yes, it's Kazuhiro Kojima.
W Sorry. Could you spell your name for me?
M Yes, it's K–A–Z–U–H–I–R–O. And my surname is K–O–J–I–M–A.
W And the other person?
M My wife.
W OK. Can I have your credit card details?
M Yes, it's a Visa card. The number is: 6053 9422 6250 9178.
W I'll just read that back to you: 6053 9422 6250 9178.
M Sorry, sorry, I meant 9187.
W And your email address, please?
M It's kaz, that's k–a–z dot kojima – all lower case – at Yahoo dot co dot j–p.
W OK, I'll send you confirmation by email today. If you need any more help, you can phone our hospitality team on 0161 868 8000.
M Can you repeat that, please?
W Sure. 0161 868 8000.
M Got it. Thank you. Goodbye.

1.6
CO = Customer, TA: Travel agent
TA W.G. Travel. How can I help you?
CO Hello, I'd like to book a fly-drive holiday to Orlando this summer.
TA Certainly. When do you want to travel?
CO The first week of August, for 10 nights.
TA OK, I'll just check for you. The cheapest adult price is departing from London Gatwick on Saturday 4th August and returning on Tuesday 14th.
CO How much is that?
TA £757.50.
CO And the child fare?
TA How old are your children?
CO They're 10 and 12.
TA OK, the child fare is £649.
CO Really, that much?
TA We have cheaper August dates with midweek fares from the 13th.
CO No thanks. We'd like to go on the 4th of August.

TA OK. Can I have your name, please?
CO Yes, it's Caitlin O'Donnell.
TA Can you spell your first name for me, please?
CO It's C–A–I–T–L–I–N.
TA And is your surname capital O, apostrophe capital D, O, double N, E, double L?
CO Yes.
TA And the names of the other passengers?
CO My husband, David, and my sons, Oscar and Noah.
TA Would you like to book accommodation as well? I can email you some of our special offers if you like.
CO Yes, please. My email is …

1.7
CO = Customer, TA: Travel agent
TA W.G.Travel. Can I help you?
CO Hello, this is Caitlin O'Donnell. I'm phoning about my reservation for Orlando. I made it yesterday. I'd like to check the cost of the flights and car hire if we go for 14 nights now. And I want to book a three-bedroom villa in Coconut Drive.
TA Is that 14 nights from early August?
CO Yes, leaving on the 4th of August and coming back on Saturday the 18th.
TA OK, let me see. Departing London Gatwick on August 4th at 09:10 a.m. and returning to the UK on Saturday 18th at 05:30 a.m. OK, the full package for four including flights, car hire and accommodation in a villa at Coconut Drive is £4,311.
CO Does that include the car insurance?
TA Yes, it does.
CO Great! Can I pay by debit card?
TA Yes, certainly. I'll just take the details …

Unit 2

2.1
1 If you want to work as a holiday rep, or resort representative, you need to be outgoing, enthusiastic, helpful, flexible, and have a professional appearance.
2 A housekeeper has to be hard-working, a good team worker, efficient and also a bit of a perfectionist.
3 It's important that a restaurant manager is organized, good at managing a team, and feels passionate about food.
4 If you want to work for a children's attraction, you should be responsible but also fun-loving and entertaining, and, most importantly, you have to like children.
5 A good tour guide is always enthusiastic, patient, communicative and a people-person.

2.2
books, checks, closes, communicates, deals, does, gives, helps, makes, organizes, plans, prepares, recommends, serves, specializes, supervises, works

2.3

I work for the Bouvier Hotel and I'm responsible for the chefs and kitchen staff. At the moment I'm planning the menu for a special dinner. The hotel is organizing a conference this week and there are four hundred and fifty people on the guest list. For special events like banquets and weddings, I often talk to the restaurant manager to make sure everything goes perfectly. Why do I love my job? Well, we always have a different menu every day, which is exciting, but it's sometimes stressful. Today, one of our deliveries is late and this morning the food and beverage manager's checking if another supplier can deliver the fish in time. All of our food needs to be fresh. People say I'm a perfectionist – I like to make sure everything is perfect. But I just enjoy helping my staff to be creative and produce dishes of a high quality. It's great when a waiter tells me our guests are enjoying their meal, or a customer says, 'This is delicious, what's in it?'

2.4

A = Afon, I = Interviewer
I So, Afon, do you have any experience as an entertainments manager?
A Yes, yes, I do. Yes, I've worked as an entertainments manager for two summers in a seaside resort in Llandudno.
I What are your responsibilities there?
A I plan and supervise entertainment for both adults and kids.
I Could you give me some examples?
A Yes, I organize karaoke, competitions, and magic shows in the evening and sport activities and day trips during the day.
I I see. And can you describe your positive qualities?
A Well, I'm friendly and outgoing and, erm ... I'm a good team worker.
I What kind of qualities does an entertainments manager need?
A That's a difficult one. I think you need to be very organized, enthusiastic and good at taking the initiative.
I Uhuh. And what do you know about Sunnyside resorts?
A They are popular family resorts and erm, you have very good reviews on the internet.
I Thank you.

Unit 3

3.1

PD – Pierre Dupont, I = Interviewer
I Do you think the tourist office offers a useful service to visitors to the city?
PD Absolutely! We're a one-stop shop, providing all the information visitors need in one place. Our multilingual staff can help visitors make the most of their holiday. They're highly trained and have an excellent knowledge of the local area.
I Do you give advice to both leisure and business travellers?
PD Yes, we provide advice to all tourists both face to face and by email and telephone. You know, Brussels is a favourite destination for congresses, events and conferences. We offer a free

service to organizers to help them plan their events, such as booking conference rooms and hotels.
I When you're not giving advice and helping tourists, what are you doing?
PD We plan new tours, seasonal events, and special festivals. It's very creative work. We write tourist information for leaflets, brochures, newsletters, press releases and, of course, our website. I also travel sometimes – you see, we organize local, national or international campaigns to promote tourism in Brussels, and go to exhibitions and holiday shows.
I What is the future of the tourist information services?
PD Digital tourism is very important now. The internet and mobile technologies are revolutionizing tourism and that includes the distribution of tourist information today.

3.2

1 It's cheaper than summer.
2 It's faster than a boat.
3 It's noisier at night.
4 It's a nicer time to visit.
5 It's as big as London.

3.3

A–E = Tourists, TIO = Tourist Infomation Officer
1
A What time do the banks open?
TIO From 8 a.m. to 2.30 p.m., Monday to Friday.
2
B Does the museum offer a group discount?
TIO Yes, groups of 15 or more get 10% off per person.
3
C How long is the walking tour?
TIO It's approximately two and a half kilometres and takes about one hour.
4
D How much is the Museum Pass?
TIO For two days it's 30 euros and for three days it's 40 euros.
5
E Do kids go free on public transport?
TIO Yes, children under 5 travel free and 5– to 15-year-olds pay child fares.

3.4

TIA = Tourist Information Assistant, T = Tourist
TIA Good morning, Galway Visitor Information Centre. This is Sháuna. How can I help you?
T Hello. Where can we stay in the area?
TIA When would you like the accommodation for?
T Tonight and tomorrow night. We can't find a bed & breakfast or hotel in the town.
TIA Yes, I understand. They're all booked up. It's because of our summer festival. It's very popular.
T What can we do?
TIA I can find accommodation for you in a village near the town. Can I have your name, sir?
T Yes, I'm Boris Malkov.
TIA Do you have a car, Mr Malkov?
T Yes, we do. We're on a motoring holiday in Ireland.

TIA Right. Well, you need to come into the office in person to book the accommodation.
T Oh, I see.
TIA Do you know how to get here? We're at number 4 High Street.
T Yes, yes. We have a map.
TIA OK, when you get here, ask for Sháuna, that's me. I'll make the booking for you.
T We'll be there in half an hour.
TIA Can I do anything else for you?
T No, no, thank you very much.
TIA You're welcome, Mr Malkov, and bye for now.

3.5

Visitor 1 The Tourist Information Centre is interesting and provides lots of useful information about the area and maps. There are lots of *Star Trek* souvenirs and clothes on sale but everything was very expensive. I bought some big plastic Vulcan ears! The town is funny with all the business signs saying Vulcan Hairdressers, Vulcan Garage and so on.
Visitor 2 We are not big *Star Trek* fans but we enjoyed the collection on display at the Vulcan Tourism & Trek Station. The Vulcan Space Adventure is an interactive exhibit where you can battle with the Klingon invaders – we had lots of fun. We also put on *Star Trek* uniforms and took pictures. The Trek Station staff are friendly and helpful and they'll take the photos for you if they aren't very busy. The gift shop has some terrific *Star Trek* souvenirs.

Unit 4

4.1

developed, continued, recorded, contributed, decreased, died, discovered, dominated, increased, modernized, played, recovered, tried, visited

4.2

The Iceni tribe, led by the legendary Queen Boadicea, destroyed the Roman city of Londinium nearly **2,000** years ago, although it was rebuilt by the Romans. Most of the crown jewels in The Tower of London date from **1661** when new ones were made for King Charles II and when they were first shown to the public.
Rat catchers and other pest controllers could not prevent epidemics of the plague. The Plague of 1664–5 killed over **100,000** Londoners.
The City is the business centre of London. England's famous architect, Christopher Wren, designed many of its buildings in the **17th** century after the Great Fire.
King George II gave number 10 Downing Street to Sir Robert Walpole in **1732**. It then became the official residence of the British Prime Minister.
In the detective stories of Sir Arthur Conan Doyle, Sherlock Holmes lived at **221b** Baker Street. But the building that is the Sherlock Holmes museum is in fact number **239**.

The Houses of Parliament were completed in **1870** but the original palace dates back to 1042. Big Ben is not the name of its world famous clock, but its **14**-tonne bell. The London Eye is a 135-metre high observation wheel which was put up to celebrate the millennium. On a clear day visitors have a **40**-kilometre view of the capital in all directions.

4.3

T1–T5 = Tourists 1–5, TG = Tour Guide
1
T1 Is a visit to platform 9¾ included in the tour?
TG Of course, a visit to platform 9¾ in King's Cross station is included.
2
T2 Excuse me. Are entrance tickets and meals included?
TG No, I'm afraid entrance tickets and meals are not included in the tour.
3
T3 Sorry to interrupt. How long do we have for lunch?
TG We have one hour for lunch, from 1 to 2 p.m.
4
T4 Excuse me. Where can I buy some souvenirs?
TG There's a shop that sells souvenirs over there next to the music store.
5
T5 Sorry, what did you say?
TG I said you can buy souvenirs in the shop over there.

4.4

TG = Tour Guide, T1 = Female Tourist, T2 = Male Tourist
G As I was saying, the castle is famous for its charm and, of course, the story that was written by Bram Stoker, the legend of Dracula. The castle dates back to 1377. Its walls are made of stone and there are many, many rooms and dark, dark corridors with secret chambers. So, follow me and don't get lost!
T1 It's a little dark in here, isn't it?
G Ah yes, that's because too much light ruins the antique paintings and furniture.
T1 And did you notice there were no mirrors anywhere?
G Did you say m, m, mirrors?
T1 Yes, I said there weren't any mirrors in the rooms or the restrooms.
G Well, we try to maintain the old traditions in Transylvania here, for authenticity. Please, no flash and don't touch the antiques!
T1 and 2 Sorry.
T2 Wow, look at this huge bed, and this old painting, Janet! It's Count Vlad ... This count looks a lot like our guide, don't you think? He's got the same eyes and moustache.
G That's very kind of you. In fact, Count Vlad is erm ..., I mean, was a distant relative, my great great great great great ... uncle. But that's enough about me. As you know, Castle Bran was a popular summer residence for the monarchs of Romania. But did you know that in 1920, Queen Mary, who was the niece of Queen Victoria of Great Britain, stayed in our beautiful

castle one summer? She fell in love with the place. The legend says her heart was kept in this silver box, which was later discovered in this very building.
T1 and 2 Really? / Ugh, no!
G I said, don't touch the antiques!
T1 Ow!
T2 What's the matter, Janet?
T1 I cut my finger on this glass.
T2 I'll go and get you something for it.
G Let me help you, my dear. Sit down for a moment. I think it's time for ... lunch!
T1 Aagh!

Unit 5

5.1

R = Receptionist, G = Guest
R Good morning. How can I help you?
G Hi, I'm here for the dentists' convention. I have a room booked. Here's my confirmation.
R Thank you. Can I see your passport or photo ID, please?
G Sure. Here you go.
R I'll just check that ... Yes, Ms Miller, a standard room for three nights.
G Does the room have a double bed?
R Yes, that's right. It's a standard double. The buffet breakfast is included in your room rate.
G Good.
R May I have your credit card, please? I'll take the details now but the hotel doesn't charge any extra costs to your card until you check out.
G OK, sure.
R Sign here, please. Thank you Ms Miller. Here's your keycard and room number. Your room is on the twelfth floor. The elevators are over there on your left. Breakfast is served from half past six until nine in the restaurant on the second floor. Would you like the bellhop to take your luggage?
G No, thanks. I'll do it myself.
R Enjoy your stay and the convention.
G Thank you.

5.2

buffet, could, guest, half, night, sign, would

5.3

1 Can I see your reservation, please?
2 May I have your credit card?
3 Could you sign here?
4 Would you like breakfast in the morning?
5 Shall I call the porter for you?

5.4

Guest 1 I travel a lot for work and the hotel serves as my office. I want all the comforts of home combined with a free wi-fi internet connection, and a big work desk in my room. A business centre is essential for printing documents, preferably one that is open 24 hours.
Guest 2 We're going to a friend's wedding in Scotland next month, and we need an affordable place to stay. We're going to be out at the celebrations all day, so we don't really need any hotel facilities

– just a comfortable bed and a clean bathroom for the weekend.
Guest 3 We're going to Tenerife again this year with the kids for some sun, sand and sea. We'll book an all-inclusive package in a good hotel that has a separate children's pool, an outdoor play area, a kids' club and some family entertainment in the evenings.
Guest 4 We're going to Paris for the weekend for our anniversary. I want luxury but don't want to stay in a big chain hotel where everything is the same, and the service is impersonal. I'd like somewhere a bit different, more stylish and intimate.

5.5

1 parking, staff, fast, shabby
2 dirty, pillow, surname, furniture
3 clean, weather, deal, sleep
4 noisy, talk, board, floor
5 view, pool, rude, towel

5.6

R = Receptionist G = Guest
R Reception.
G Hello, this is Mr Talbot in room 316.
R Good morning, Mr Talbot. How can I help you?
G Our room is very noisy. I couldn't sleep with the sound of the sea all last night.
R Really? May I ask, did you close your window?
G No, no, we always sleep with the window open. We don't like air-conditioning.
R Oh, I see. Would you like to move to a room at the back of the hotel?
G Do they have a sea view?
R I'm afraid not. The rooms overlook the hotel gardens and pool.
G Well, that's not good enough. We want a sea view.
R I'm very sorry for the inconvenience. I can arrange for an electric fan for your room tonight. Then you could close the window.
G I'm not sure; a fan can be noisy too. Hmm. Well, OK then. I hope I get a better night's sleep tonight.

5.7

Speaker 1 A lot of the reception staff are young and inexperienced, and they need to learn how to be more polite and friendly sometimes.
Speaker 2 I don't know what to show them, and I can't drive and answer all the guests' questions. I'm not a safari guide.
Speaker 3 I gave the guest a brochure with all the times and prices for our excursions. The thing is, it's from last year because we haven't had time to print the new one.
Speaker 4 He ordered one thing and then he changed his mind. I'm the only person on night duty and it was a very busy evening.
Speaker 5 We don't have enough new mosquito nets or towels. We also need some better products to clean the bathrooms.

Unit 6

6.1

apple, banana, beef, cabbage, carp, carrot, chicken, cod, cucumber, duck, lamb, mango, onion, orange, pineapple, potato, rabbit, salmon, trout, tuna

6.2

W = Waiter, S = Sarah, D = David
W Would you like some drinks before you order your meal?
S Yes please. I'll have a sparkling water with some ice.
D A tonic water for me, please. I don't want any ice.
W Certainly, I'll get your drinks.
S There aren't many customers in here.
D It's still early. I expect there'll be lots of people later.
S And there aren't many meat dishes on the menu.
D It's a seafood restaurant Sarah! There are lots of fish dishes.
S Well, we haven't got much time. Let's order when the waiter comes back.
D Good idea. Fresh cod sounds good!

6.3

W = Waiter, C1 = Customer 1, C2 = Customer 2
C2 Excuse me, waiter?
W I'll be with you in just a moment.
C1 They're busy in here, aren't they?
C2 Yeah, very busy.
W Sorry to keep you waiting. Are you ready to order?
C1 Not quite. I can't decide on the starter. What is *Pulpo a la Gallega*?
W That's octopus. It's boiled, sliced and then sprinkled with paprika, salt and olive oil.
C1 Oh, I see. And the *Gambas Ajillo*?
W That's prawns, cooked in olive oil with lots of garlic and chilli.
C1 Prawns?
C2 They're what we call 'shrimp' in the States.
C1 Ah! Shrimp. Sounds nice and garlicky.
C2 And spicy.
C1 I'll have those.
W An excellent choice. And for you, sir?
C2 What are the *Verduras a la parrilla*?
W That's grilled mixed vegetables: aubergine, courgette, red peppers and mushrooms.
C1 I don't think I know some of those vegetables. Hold on, aren't aubergines what we call 'eggplant', and courgette is 'zucchini', right?
C2 You got it. I'll have the grilled vegetables.
C1 Let's share our starters.
C2 Good idea.
W And for the main course?
C2 We'd like paella for two.
C1 What exactly is in the *Paella Marinera*?
W That's our seafood paella. It's made with rice, prawns, mussels, clams, squid and sea bass.
C1 Can we have it without the mussels?
W Without the mussels?
C1 It's not that I'm allergic. It's just I don't like the look of mussels.
W OK, I'll make a note for the chef. Would you like some more bread?
C1 Yes, please.

6.4

1 Would you like to order now?
2 Can I have the menu in English?
3 I'll have the chicken salad.
4 Would you like some desserts?
5 We'd like the bill, please.
6 Did you enjoy your meal?

6.5

Diner 1 Our personal chef made the experience very enjoyable. He was very entertaining and funny and made us laugh. He was like a samurai warrior with the knife!
Diner 2 The best dish is the tuna steak with teriyaki sauce, which is delicious. The rest was just OK.
Diner 3 The set menu sounds cheap but when you add on drinks, side orders, the twelve and a half percent service charge, the bill came to nearly £100 for two! The drinks are really overpriced.
Diner 4 I went with colleagues from work. When you arrive people are laughing and having a great time. But the music was very loud and with all the cooking it was difficult to talk.
Diner 5 We booked but waited for ages for our table, and then we had to wait another hour till the chef arrived to start cooking.

6.6

O = Owner, F = Front of House Manager
O Some diners say that we're not good value for money, but most people are happy about the quality of the food and the prices.
F Let's give them some more complimentary dishes with the meals. I mean, a salad and some grilled vegetables are cheap enough and people love to feel they're getting something for nothing.
O True. I think we'll have to do something about the service charge.
F Won't that reduce the staff's tips?
O Yes, but twelve and a half percent is very high and, you know, I think the customers should decide how much they want to leave as a reward for service.
F Yes, well, the staff are always complaining about their low wages. If we do that ...
O OK, OK, let's just reduce the charge to say, ten percent?
F I don't think that's a good idea.
O Well, OK, we'll think about that one some more. Next point, the drinks, how about a sort of happy hour?
F Yes, we don't get many diners in early evening; we could offer two for the price of one on drinks before 6 o'clock.
O I think that could work. And you need to keep an eye on the volume of the music and remember to turn it down as more people come in and the place gets noisy.
F Will do. And we get a lot of complaints about the slow service, especially at the weekends. I think it's because there aren't enough staff. We could employ a few more waiters, especially for the Friday and Saturday evening shifts and Sunday lunch. What do you think?
O Erm ... that sounds as if it's going to cost me money.

Unit 7

7.1

A = Alicia, T = Tom
A So, what are your holiday plans, Tom?
T Well, I'm going to Brazil with my wife.
A That's exciting! How long are you going for?
T It's a two-week tour.
A Are you flying to Rio de Janeiro?
T That's right.
A Do you know anyone in Rio?
T No, but the travel rep will meet us at the airport. And we're staying in a hotel that's 200 m from the beach.
A Great! So, I suppose you'll visit Sugarloaf mountain, and the streets where the famous carnival takes place.
T Yes, and we just want to relax on Copacabana beach. We're going to play volleyball, go surfing or sunbathe.
A Oh, if you like people-watching, you'll love Copacabana beach! And where are you going after Rio?
T Well, for the second part of the tour we're flying out to the city of Foz do Iguaçu, you know, to see the Iguaçu Falls. The agent says you can see the falls from both the Brazilian and the Argentinian side.
A That's right. I've heard they're spectacular.
T And then we're going to the Amazon rainforest.
A And how are you getting there?
T Let me check the itinerary. Let's see, it says here we're flying to Manaus and staying in the Amazon for five days. It's basic lodge accommodation and, apparently, the showers aren't very warm, but that won't be a problem in the jungle.
A No. And I'm sure you'll enjoy it, going trekking and wildlife spotting. And what are you going to do after the Amazon?
T After that we're flying on to Salvador de Bahia where we're staying for four days. Sorry, no, the agent told us we're going to stay there for six days.
A And where are you going to stay in Salavador?
T It'll be a comfortable four-star hotel where we can relax by the pool, or rent bikes and go cycling.
A Fantastic. I'm sure you'll have a great time!
T Yes, I can't wait.

7.2

bay, cliff, coast, desert, lake, reef, plain, river, valley, waterfall

7.3

Example It's best to go in summer.
1 I'd like to tell you about our beautiful parks.
2 Then I'm going to show you some photos.
3 You'll see some fantastic scenery.
4 As you can see, the scenery's spectacular.
5 Now, I'll show you the islands.
6 It's best to go skiing in the spring.

7.4

Speaker 1 When we arrived at Kochi, there was no one to meet us – our train was very late, so we had to get to the hotel on our own, which took us forever.

Speaker 2 The tour guide told us we would see lots of wild animals at the Periyar Wildlife sanctuary, but we only saw a couple of elephants.

Speaker 3 They took us to see the spice plantations but, to be honest, they were a bit boring after visiting the tea plantations two days before that.

Speaker 4 They said Alappuzha is famous for its houseboats and boat races. It was lovely staying on a houseboat but it was disappointing because there weren't any boat races the week we were there.

Speaker 5 At the end of our stay in Kochi, we had to go to see a performance of Kathakali dance. But I'm not very interested in folk dancing and I was very tired on the last day – I think it's better to include some more free time in a tour like this one.

Unit 8

8.1

P = Passenger, IA = Information Assistant

P Excuse me, can you tell me how to get to central London by public transport? My hotel's near Victoria Station.

IA Certainly. At this time of night, you have two options. You can take the Heathrow Express train to Paddington. It's a non-stop service that leaves every 15 minutes and takes 15 minutes. Then take the underground from there to Victoria.

P How much does that cost?

IA The fare is £19.00 single and £34 for a return ticket. But that doesn't include the underground.

P Wow! It's not cheap, is it?

IA Alternatively, you can take the Piccadilly line tube to Green Park. Then take a Victoria line tube south one stop.

P How long does it take?

IA About an hour.

P And the fare?

IA A single is £5.50 to central London zones.

P That sounds more reasonable. Where's the underground station?

IA Just go straight on past the car hire offices and follow the signs. Then take the escalators or the lift down to the lower ground floor. It's about five minutes on the moving walkway.

P Can I buy my ticket here?

IA No, you get that at the ticket office or in the machines there. There are often long queues for the tickets.

P I see.

IA The last tube leaves in about 25 minutes, so you should go now.

P Oh, right. Many thanks for your help.

8.2

1 Passengers should get to the airport early.

2 You can't take drinks through security.

3 You don't have to pay for the trolleys.

4 Passengers shouldn't lock their check-in baggage.

5 You are only allowed to have one carry-on bag.

6 Your passport mustn't expire during your visit to the country.

7 Passengers can buy tax-free items after clearing security control.

8.3

1 Passengers can check in online.

2 You can't fly without a passport.

3 **A** Can I have a window seat?
  B Yes, you can.

4 You can go through security now.

5 I can't book you on the next flight.

6 I'm sorry, we can't find your bag.

7 You can't take that bag on board, I'm afraid.

8.4

M = Man, W = Woman

M Good morning madam. How can I help you?

W I think my luggage is lost. All the other passengers have collected their bags and gone.

M OK, can I have your flight details please?

W I was on the Athens flight. We arrived an hour ago.

M Can I see your baggage receipt?

W Baggage receipt? What's that?

M It's a little label they gave you when you checked in. It might be on your passport.

W Ah, yes, here it is.

M Thank you. Can you describe your baggage for me?

W It's a black suitcase.

M A black suitcase. Yes, we get a lot of those. Anything special about the suitcase?

W No, it was just a normal black suitcase.

M OK, and you say it wasn't at carousel 5.

W Carousel 5? I didn't look at carousel 5. I was at number 6.

M Ah, well the baggage from your flight was on carousel 5.

W Whoops! Sorry. I'll go and look for it. Thanks.

M You're welcome.

8.5

1 go: close, no, how, slow

2 near: we're, here, date, year

3 pay: wait, clear, plane, train

4 toilet: right, noisy, coin, enjoy

5 air: airport, fare, there, sign

6 my: flight, licence, eight, aisle

7 out: lounge, phone, hour, allowed

8 tour: euro, sure, Europe, don't

8.6

I = Interviewer, P = Purser

I What skills and personal characteristics do you need to be a flight attendant?

P The cabin crew have to be confident, friendly and diplomatic. You need to be polite but firm when dealing with difficult people. You have to stay calm under pressure and in emergencies. If a passenger is very rude or demanding, keep your emotions and your voice under control. You also need to be sensitive towards people who are anxious or upset.

I Do you often have to deal with difficult situations?

P Absolutely. I meet around 500 people every day and difficult situations happen all the time. One of the most disturbing is when you discover that a passenger is smoking in the toilet. This is a serious danger for the passengers' safety and it's punishable by a fine. In this case, we have to inform the police and stop the passenger from leaving the aircraft until they arrive.

Unit 9

9.1

1 No, they haven't cleaned the third floor yet.

2 He's gone to the laundry room.

3 Yes, she's had a break.

4 Yes, I've counted the hangers.

5 No, he hasn't checked the towels yet.

6 Yes, we've washed the towels.

7 Yes, I've talked to the supervisor.

8 No, she hasn't ironed her uniform.

9.2

asked, checked, cleaned, counted, finished, inspected, ironed, phoned, repaired, supervised, talked, washed

9.3

I = Interviewer, D = Davis Langdon

I In today's programme we're talking about hotel refurbishment with Davis Langdon. Mr Langdon, we've seen how some projects mean hotels close down for long periods of time. How can a hotel make sure that there is minimal disruption during refurbishment?

D Ideally, refurbishment is done in a number of phases, or stages, and this involves closing down complete floors to minimize disruption. It's important about one third of the work is done in any one phase to maintain continuity. It's also important that the contractors, the builders and interior designers, and everyone working on the project, have a good relationship with the hotel management. They need to work fast, often working maybe six or seven days a week, so that the hotel doesn't lose money.

I Of course, this is the most difficult part for hoteliers, closing down rooms, or complete floors. How long can refurbishment take?

D Well, a simple project takes about 10–12 weeks, but remodelling and bigger projects can take 4–5 months, or longer. Coordination is very important, and complicated, especially when working on bathroom fittings. And, of course, any noisy work has to be done during the day, not at night, and guests must have safe access to their rooms and be able to use most of the hotel facilities during this time. But safety comes first.

I I see. And what advice can you give to hoteliers who are planning to refurbish?

D Well, you have to know the exact date for completion and to be sure that there are absolutely no defects or problems. So guests can occupy rooms and hotel operations can return back to normal as soon as possible.

I Thank you very much, Davis Langdon.

9.4

design, designer, extend, extension, furniture, innovation, lobby, refurbish, renovate, renovation, restore, restoration, stylish

9.5

G = Guest, R = Receptionist

G Hi, we'd like to check out, please.

R Good morning. May I have your name, please?

G It's Fernando de la Cruz.

R Ah, yes. Here's your folio. You pre-paid one night, that's $174, so the balance due is $274. Could you enter your PIN here?

G Sure.

R How was your stay with us?

G Great. We loved the suite. But we couldn't use the spa on our first night because it was closed.

R I'm sorry to hear that. I'm afraid the spa closes at 9 p.m. Here's your receipt. Would you like me to order you a taxi?

G No, thanks. Your colleague ordered one this morning.

R OK, we look forward to seeing you again. Bye!

9.6

Let's see, the first security measure, install security cameras in all guest rooms and public areas. Well, we already have security cameras in public areas like the parking lot, the lobby and the elevators, but we can't have cameras in the guests' rooms – that's an invasion of their privacy.

I think contracting more security staff is a good idea. We usually have a security guard at nights, for the guests' and employees' safety, but perhaps we should make sure there are one or two guards during the daytime, too.

I don't think we can adopt the third option, ask guests to go through a security check – most guests wouldn't like the idea of an airport-style security check in a hotel. And it isn't good for public relations to suggest that guests might steal from the hotel during their stay.

Then there's the idea of declaring an amnesty. I've heard there's a famous hotel in Ottawa in Canada that's done that and asked past guests to return items. You know, no questions asked. They didn't want guests to give back ordinary items

like towels or sheets, but some relatives of past guests returned valuable things like silver spoons and antique glasses.

Of course we can't hire private detectives to follow guests – that's an extreme measure. But I definitely agree with the final option: in serious cases you should immediately report any suspicious guests to the local police if you think they have done something illegal. That is what happened when we suspected a cleaning firm was stealing from the hotel.

Unit 10

10.1

T = Tourist, SA = Shop assistant

SA Can I help you, madam?

T Yes, how much is that white beach dress?

SA 50 TRY.

T Fifteen?

SA No, fifty. 5–0.

T Oh, no thanks.

SA Wait a moment. We have an offer today of two for the price of one.

T Two for one?

SA That's right. You can choose any colour: black, white, blue, red ...

T All right. Do you have a white one in a medium? And I think I'll have a black one, too.

SA Medium size? Sure. And for only 65 TRY, I'll give you a third dress. How does that sound?

T Three for sixty-five?

SA Yes, which colour would you like? Red, blue, turquoise? They're great in hot weather, and they wash very well.

T The turquoise one looks lovely. I think I'll take a turquoise one for my friend. Small.

SA Here you are. That'll be 65 TRY all together, please.

10.2

R1 = Receptionist 1, R2 = Receptionist 2

R1 So, I was thinking that if we swap shifts next weekend, I'll be able to go away with my family.

R2 Sorry, I can't change with you next weekend. I'm going to my friend's party.

R1 Yes, but I swapped with you last month when you were going to a party. If you ask me to change my shift for you, then you should swap with me. It's only fair.

R2 I'm sorry, but I can't do it this time. It's a birthday party. All my friends are going.

R1 All right. When you ask me for a favour next time, I won't swap with you!

R2 There's no need to get angry, Claire. Look, if you ask the manager, I'm sure she'll cover for you.

10.3

A = Alice, D = Darren, EM = Events manager

A So, we'd like menu number 4, please.

EM How many guests are you planning to invite?

A About 120.

D How much is that going to cost us?

EM Let's see, menu 4 is £85 per head. If you invite 120 guests, it'll cost £10,200.

D What about menu 5? There's salad, chicken and ice cream. Sounds good. How much is that one?

A If we serve people chicken and salad, they'll say we're cheap! Menu 4 sounds much better, Darren.

EM Well, it's certainly more economical at £70 per person. But then you will only have three courses, not four.

D Yes, but it'll cost us less. What's 70 by 120?

EM Let's see ... If you choose menu 5, that'll be £8,400. So, that's a difference of erm ... £1,800.

A People will laugh if we serve them chicken and salad at our wedding!

EM Would you like a moment together to discuss this?

10.4

1 If you take this lovely scarf, I'll give you the lot for 75 lira.

2 How much will it be if I buy another dress?

3 If you ask Amanda nicely, perhaps she'll work your shift next weekend.

4 I'll swap with you the following weekend if that helps.

5 If you don't invite all your cousins, I'll agree to a more expensive menu.

6 We'll be able to afford a better menu if your mother doesn't invite all her friends.

7 How much will it cost if we choose menu 4 and have 110 guests?

8 If you decide on menu 4 and 110 guests, it'll come to £9,300.

10.5

Speaker 1 My city is the centre of the Hindi film industry, known as Bollywood. It's also a shopper's paradise with exclusive boutiques, ethnic markets and mini-bazaars. There are fast food stalls on almost every street, but also great restaurants, theatres, cinemas, and cafés. I'm not sure of the official slogan at the moment but like New York, we say it's a city that never sleeps. A good tourism slogan should tell you something about the place, so I like, 'Mumbai: Film, shopping and fun!'

Speaker 2 Some people say our capital is a cold city, and not just because of the weather. This year our tourism board wanted to create a new marketing campaign that shows our capital has heart, and a smile for visitors, too. At the agency where I work, we want to communicate that you won't just find impressive attractions like the Kremlin. It is also one of the most expensive cities in the world: we have the most billionaires, the most expensive cups of coffee, and the best nightlife. So, I've thought of, 'Moscow: Magnificent – with love!' What do you think?

Speaker 3 Cities like New York, Las Vegas and San Francisco have had great tourism slogans, but now the Convention and Visitors Authority have created a new multi-million dollar marketing campaign to show visitors what the country has to offer. It should highlight the idea of shows, shopping and dining. A colleague suggested, 'The greatest show on earth'! But it also needs to communicate the concept that we're a huge country and we like to do things on a big scale, so how about something like 'The USA: The bigger, the better!'?

ANSWER KEY

Unit 1

GRAMMAR AND VOCABULARY, PAGE 4

Exercise 1

-n	-ian	-ish	-ese	other
Australian German (North) American	Italian	British Spanish	Chinese	French

Exercise 2

Australia: Australian

Britain: British

China: Chinese

France: French

Germany: German

Italy: Italian

Spain: Spanish

USA: American

Exercise 3

-n	-ian	-ish	-ese	other
Indian Kenyan Korean Mexican Russian	Brazilian Canadian Norwegian	Irish Polish Turkish	Japanese Portuguese	Greek Thai Dutch

Exercise 4

1 T

2 F (fewer than 10% of outbound trips are to Europe and the USA.)

3 T

4 F (They generally like to spend money on luxury brands.)

5 F (They prefer travelling in tour groups of 30–40 people.)

Exercise 5

1 art gallery (Attractions)

2 golf (Recreation and entertainment)

3 business convention (Events and conferences)

4 car hire (Transportation)

5 bistro (Food and beverage)

6 hostel (Accommodation)

Exercise 6

1 d Where is the Louvre museum?

2 f How many visitors does the museum get?

3 a How big is the Louvre's collection?

4 b What is the top attraction?

5 e How much does it cost to visit the museum?

6 c How long is the guided tour?

Exercise 7

1 What's / What is

2 How many …does

3 What are

4 When is / When's

5 How often do

6 What do you

PROFESSIONAL SKILLS, PAGE 6

Exercise 1

/eɪ/: A, H, J, K

/iː/: B, C, D, E, G, P, T, V (Z* – US Eng)

/e/: F, L, M, N, S, X, Z

/aɪ/: I, Y

/əʊ/: O

/uː/: Q, U, W

/ɑː/: R

Exercise 2

1 Friday 16th March

2 9 a.m. / 9 o'clock

3 11.07 a.m.

4 Sunday 18th March

5 18.15h / 6.15 p.m.

6 20.27h / 8.27 p.m.

7 £80.20

8 £160.40

Exercise 3

1 Single		5 fare	
2 one-way		6 later train	
3 When do		7 6 p.m.	
4 So that's		8 How would	

Exercise 4

1 Saturday 17th March at 1.30 p.m.

2 £290 + 20% VAT

3 Mr & Mrs Kazuhiro Kojima

4 6053–9422–6250–9187

5 kaz.kojima@yahoo.co.jp

6 0161 868 8000

Exercise 5

1 have

2 spell

3 details

4 back

5 meant

6 repeat

CASE STUDY, PAGE 7

Exercise 1

1 OR / AL   **4** AL

2 AL   **5** OR / AL

3 OR

Exercise 2

1 10

2 Saturday 4th August

3 Tuesday 14th August

4 £757.50

5 £649

6 Caitlin and David O'Donnell

7 Oscar and Noah O'Donnell

8 (special offers on) accommodation

Exercise 3

Return date: ~~Tuesday 14th August~~ Saturday 18th August

Total duration: ~~10~~ 14 nights

Fly-drive ~~only - no~~ and accommodation (three-bedroom villa in Coconut Drive)

~~Not inc.~~ Included Car insurance

Total price: ~~£4,133~~ £4,311

Payment made by ~~credit~~ debit card. Thank you.

Unit 2

GRAMMAR AND VOCABULARY, PAGE 8

Exercise 1

Across

2 bellboy (also bellhop)

4 concierge

8 waiter

9 flight attendant

10 housekeeper

Down

1 receptionist

3 travel agent

5 chef

6 guide

7 entertainer

Exercise 2

1 ski instructor (Recreation and entertainment)

2 events manager (Events and conferences)

3 concierge (Accommodation)

4 museum guide (Attractions)

5 executive chef (Food and beverage)

6 pilot (Transportation)

Exercise 3

1 flexible; professional

2 hardworking; efficient

3 organized; passionate

4 responsible; entertaining

5 enthusiastic; communicative

Exercise 4

/z/: deals, does, gives, plans, prepares, recommends, serves

/ɪz/: closes, organizes, specializes, supervises

/s/: books, checks, communicates, helps, makes, works

Exercise 5

1 's working; 's ringing

2 's having; 're giving

3 's planning; 's asking

4 's preparing 's supervising

Exercise 6

a 3   **b** 1   **c** 4   **d** 2

Exercise 7

c

Exercise 8

1 work; 'm
2 'm planning
3 's organizing; are
4 often talk; goes
5 's checking
6 tells; are enjoying

PROFESSIONAL SKILLS, PAGE 10

Exercise 1

1 Personal details
2 Profile
3 Education and qualifications
4 Work experience
5 Volunteer experience
6 Additional information
7 Interests
8 References

Exercise 2

(i) a **(ii)** b **(iii)** c

Exercise 3

c

CASE STUDY, PAGE 11

Exercise 1

1 b **2** c **3** d

Job title a is not used.

Exercise 2

1 writing
2 attached
3 for
4 passionate
5 studying
6 experience
7 responsible
8 outgoing
9 team
10 see
11 look
12 faithfully

Exercise 3

The interviewer asks questions 1, 3, 4, 6, and 8.

Exercise 4

1 summers; resort
2 plan; supervise
3 friendly; worker

Unit 3

GRAMMAR AND VOCABULARY, PAGE 12

Exercise 1

1 In the Grand-Place, the central square
2 9 a.m.–6 p.m.
3 Nothing, it's a free service.
4 €34
5 trams, buses and metro

Exercise 2

1 day trips
2 make the most of
3 see the sights
4 vouchers
5 admission
6 unlimited

Exercise 3

The correct order is d, c, e, b, a.

Exercise 4

1 d **2** a **3** e **4** c **5** b

Exercise 5

1 ~~most~~ more expensive
2 ~~far~~ further from / farther from
3 cold ~~that~~ as
4 larger ~~that~~ than
5 the ~~worse~~ worst

Exercise 6

1 richer
2 higher than
3 earliest
4 most remote
5 most unusual
6 the easiest
7 best
8 high as
9 most beautiful
10 the largest

Exercise 7

1 isolated (*remote* is also correct)
2 adventurous
3 poorer (in pocket)
4 tiny
5 gigantic
6 carved
7 stunning
8 unique

Exercise 8

1 4 words: It's cheaper than summer.
2 5 words: It's faster than a boat.
3 4 words: It's noisier at night.
4 6 words: It's a nicer time to visit.
5 5 words: It's as big as London.

Exercise 9

1 It's <u>cheaper</u> than <u>summer</u>.

2 It's <u>faster</u> than a <u>boat</u>.

3 It's <u>noisier</u> at <u>night</u>.

4 It's a <u>nicer</u> <u>time</u> to <u>visit</u>.

5 It's as <u>big</u> as <u>London</u>.

PROFESSIONAL SKILLS, PAGE 14

Exercise 1

1 a: 8 a.m. to 2.30 p.m.

2 d: 15 or more; 10% off per person

3 c: 2.5 km long; 1 hour

4 b: 2 days: 30 euros; 3 days: 40 euros

5 e: children under 5; 5 to 15

Exercise 2

1 He wants to find accommodation in the town.

2 The summer festival.

3 Reserve / book accommodation for him in a nearby village.

4 Boris Malkov.

5 By car – he's on a motoring holiday in Ireland.

6 Come into the tourist office to book the accommodation in person.

Exercise 3

(correct answers **bold**)

1 **This is** Sháuna. **How** can I help you?

2 When **would you like** the accommodation for?

3 Can I have your **name**, sir?

4 You need to **come into** the office in person to book the accommodation.

5 I'll make the **booking** for you.

6 **Can I do** anything else **for you**?

Exercise 4

1 d **2** f **3** b **4** e **5** a **6** c

CASE STUDY, PAGE 15

Exercise 1

c

Exercise 2

1 fans

2 on display

3 virtual reality (game)

4 self-guided

Exercise 3

1 Visitor 2

2 Visitors 1 and 2

3 Visitor 1

4 Visitor 2

5 Visitor 2

Exercise 4

1 The information about the area and maps.

2 The souvenirs and clothes in the gift shop were expensive.

3 The collection on display, the virtual reality game, the gift shop.

4 *Star Trek* uniforms.

5 They can take photos of you in your uniform.

Exercise 5

1 c **2** a **3** d **4** b **5** f **6** e

Entertainment: 3d; 5f

Gift shop: 1c; 6e

Special events: 2a; 4b

Unit 4

GRAMMAR AND VOCABULARY, PAGE 16

Exercise 1

1 development **4** tailored

2 transfer **3** art

3 sandy **6** architecture

Exercise 2

1 -d **2** i **3** vowel

Exercise 3

1 discovered **7** modernized

2 died **8** contributed

3 played **9** visited

4 dominated **10** increased

5 tried **11** decreased

6 developed **12** recovered

Exercise 4

/t/: decreased, developed, increased

/d/: continued, died, discovered, modernized, played, recovered, tried

/ɪd/: contributed, dominated, recorded, visited

Exercise 5

1 Shopping mall: the others are government buildings.

2 Pillar: the others are tourist attractions and complete buildings.

3 Pyramid: the others are places where people live.

4 Building: the others are parts of a building.

5 Classical: the others are landmarks or places.

6 French, which is a nationality: the others are periods of history used as names for styles of art and architecture.

Exercise 6

1 Who designed the Houses of Parliament?

2 Who was the first monarch to live in Buckingham Palace?

3 Where did Charles Dickens write the book, *Oliver Twist*?

4 Where did Shakespeare produce his plays?

5 Which London museum was renamed in memory of Prince Albert?

6 When did Harrods, the famous department store, first open?

Exercise 7

a 5 **b** 3 **c** 2 **d** 6 **e** 4 **f** 1

Exercise 8

1 destroyed **7** designed

2 was rebuilt **8** gave

3 were made **9** became

4 shown **10** lived

5 could not (couldn't) **11** were completed

6 killed **12** was put up

Exercise 9

a 2,000 **f** 221b

b 1661 **g** 239

c 100,000 **h** 1870

d 17th **i** 14

e 1732 **j** 40

PROFESSIONAL SKILLS, PAGE 18

Exercise 1

1 b **2** a **3** f **4** c **5** d **6** e

Exercise 2

1 BS **2** HP **3** BS **4** BS **5** HP **6** HP

Exercise 3

1 Is a visit to platform 9¾ included in the tour?

2 Are entrance tickets and meals included?

3 How long do we have for lunch?

4 Where can I buy some souvenirs? / Is there a souvenir shop near here?

5 Sorry, what did you say? / Could / Can you repeat that please?

CASE STUDY, PAGE 19

Exercise 1

1 Tour description

2 Duration

3 Tour itinerary

4 Price

5 Not included

Exercise 2

1 F (it's mostly famous for the story of Dracula)

2 T

3 T

4 F (it's dark because too much light damages the paintings)

5 F (he looks like the guide)

6 T

Exercise 3

1 for **5** in

2 to **6** in

3 of **7** for

4 in **8** for

Exercise 4

a 5 **b** 2 **c** 8 **d** 6 **e** 4 **f** 1 **g** 7 **h** 3

Unit 5

GRAMMAR AND VOCABULARY, PAGE 20

Exercise 1

The correct order is c, a, h, f, e, b, d, g

Exercise 2

1 For a (dentist's) convention.

2 A double bed.

3 At check out.

4 On the twelfth floor.

5 From 6.30 a.m. to 9 a.m.

6 In the restaurant on the second floor.

Exercise 3

1 Can I

2 I'll just

3 buffet breakfast

4 May I

5 Sign

6 Here's

7 Would you

8 Enjoy your stay

Exercise 4

1 buffet: *t* is silent

2 could: *l* is silent

3 guest: *u* is silent

4 half: *l* is silent

5 night: *gh* are silent

6 sign: *g* is silent

7 would: *l* is silent

Exercise 5

1 Can I see your reservation, please?

2 May I have your credit card?

3 Could you sign here?

4 Would you like breakfast in the morning?

5 Shall I call the porter for you?

Exercise 6

Offers and requests are essentially *yes/no* questions. The speaker's intonation usually rises at the end of these questions to sound polite. It also rises on *please*. If the intonation falls on *please* it makes it sound more serious. The speaker's voice also rises on key content words.

Exercise 7

1 d   2 c   3 a   4 b   5 f   6 h   7 e   8 g

Hotel services and facilities: 3a; 4b; 7e; 8g

Room facilities: 1d; 2c; 5f; 6h

Exercise 8

1 in-room safe

2 front desk

3 laundry service

4 baby cot

5 walk-in shower

6 swimming pool

Exercise 9

1 walk-in

2 queen

3 familiar

4 wi-fi

5 in-room

6 breakfast

Exercise 10

bed: blanket, duvet, mattress, pillow, sheet

bathroom: shampoo, shower gel, soap, toiletries, towel

business centre: computer, fax, photocopier, printer, scanner

Exercise 11

1 hostel

2 business

3 boutique

4 budget

5 resort

6 luxury

Exercise 12

1 business hotel

2 budget hotel

3 resort hotel

4 boutique hotel

PROFESSIONAL SKILLS, PAGE 22

Exercise 1

1 uncomfortable

2 inefficient

3 inexperienced

4 unfriendly

5 unhappy

6 unhelpful

7 disorganized

8 impolite

Exercise 2

1 b   2 a   3 d   4 f   5 e   6 c

Exercise 3

1 shabby

2 pillow

3 weather

4 noisy

5 towel

Exercise 4

1 b   2 c   3 a   4 a   5 b

Exercise 5

1 for

2 at

3 about

4 with

5 at

6 to

7 at

8 with

9 for

10 on

CASE STUDY, PAGE 23

Exercise 1

1 c **2** b **3** f **4** a **5** e **6** d

Exercise 2

Speaker 1 the reception manager

Speaker 2 the excursion driver

Speaker 3 the concierge

Speaker 4 the room service waiter

Speaker 5 the housekeeper

Exercise 3

1 c **2** f **3** a **4** e **5** b **6** d

Unit 6

GRAMMAR AND VOCABULARY, PAGE 24

Exercise 1

Meat: beef, chicken, duck, lamb, rabbit

Fish: carp, cod, salmon, trout, tuna

Fruit: apple, banana, mango, orange, pineapple

Vegetables: cabbage, carrot, cucumber, onion, potato

Exercise 2

1 b **2** f **3** d **4** e **5** a **6** c

Note: On the CD–ROM you can hear the British English and American English pronunciations of the word by clicking on the audio symbols. You can also hear the example sentence by clicking on the audio symbol beside it.

Exercise 3

O: beef, carp, cod, duck, lamb, trout

Oo: apple, cabbage, carrot, chicken, mango, onion, orange, rabbit, salmon, tuna

Ooo: cucumber, pineapple

oOo: banana, potato

Note the pronunciation of the words with silent letters, e.g. *lamb* (*b* is silent), *salmon* (*l* is silent)

Exercise 4

1 dairy products: cereal is a grain product

2 grain products: mint is a herb

3 beverages: squid is seafood

4 shellfish: tea is a beverage

5 herbs and spices: ketchup is a condiment

6 condiments: ice cream is a dairy product

Exercise 5

-*s*: chefs, customers, guests, meals, orders, vegetables

-*es* : businesses, glasses, lunches, mangoes, potatoes, waitresses

-*ies*: anniversaries

other: knives, men, women

Exercise 6

1 party **5** sandwiches

2 company **6** tomatoes

3 children **7** dishes

4 people **8** allergies

Exercise 7

1 some (use *some* in questions that are offers)

2 some

3 any

4 many

5 lots

6 many (*any* is also possible, though less likely)

7 lots

8 much

Exercise 8

Across		Down	
3	set	**1**	waiter
5	bill	**2**	glass
8	specials	**3**	station
9	knife	**4**	tips
10	booking	**6**	cutlery
12	dessert	**7**	napkin
14	covers	**11**	order
		13	run

PROFESSIONAL SKILLS, PAGE 26

Exercise 1

1 Hungary **7** sprinkled

2 made **8** served with

3 seasoned **9** spicy

4 added **10** Korea

5 Iraqi **11** made of

6 marinated **12** side dish

Exercise 2

1 octopus **7** Grilled

2 salt **8** aubergine

3 olive oil **9** courgette

4 prawns **10** Seafood

5 garlic **11** mussels

6 chilli **12** clams

The woman orders the prawns (*Gambas Ajillo*) for her starter.

The man orders the grilled mixed vegetables (*Verdura a la Parilla*) for his starter.

They want seafood paella (*Paella Marinera*) for the main course, without mussels.

Exercise 3

1 c (*b* is not polite)

2 a (*c* is not polite)

3 b (*a* is not polite)

4 a (*c* is not polite)

Exercise 4

1 Would you like to order now? W

2 Can I have the menu in English? D

3 I'll have the chicken salad. D

4 Would you like some desserts? W

5 We'd like the bill, please. D

6 Did you enjoy your meal? W

CASE STUDY, PAGE 27

Exercise 1

1 Japanese

2 8

3 Vegetarian and low-calorie.

4 The chefs preparing and cooking the food.

5 Families and (noisy) parties.

6 Sunday lunchtime because there is a children's special menu on offer.

Exercise 2

1 –friendly

2 highchairs

3 multi-course

4 diners

5 (good) value for money

6 appetizer

7 clientele

8 parties

Exercise 3

The restaurant needs to improve on the price of the food and drink, the noisy level and the waiting time for a table.

1 Diner 2

2 Diner 1

3 Diner 3

4 Diner 5

5 Diner 4

Exercise 4

1 a salad, (some) grilled vegetables

2 service charge, 10%

3 two for the price, 6 p.m.

4 volume of the music, turn it down

5 waiters, evening shifts

Unit 7

GRAMMAR AND VOCABULARY, PAGE 28

Exercise 1

1 fifth largest

2 South America

3 Atlantic Ocean

4 mountain ranges

5 lowest point

6 Major rivers

7 tropical forest

8 animal species

Exercise 2

1 Stay in Rio de Janeiro

2 See the Iguaçu Falls

3 Visit the Amazon rainforest

4 Fly to Salvador de Bahia

Exercise 3

1 b **2** c **3** c **4** b **5** a **6** a

Exercise 4

Sea: bay, coast, reef

Fresh water: lake, river, waterfall

Land: cliff, desert, plain, valley

Exercise 5

bay, cliff, coast, <u>de</u>sert, lake, plain, reef, river, <u>vall</u>ey, <u>wa</u>terfall

Exercise 6

/e/: desert

/ɪ/: cliff, river

/iː/: reef

/æ/: valley

/ɔː/: waterfall

/eɪ/: bay, lake, plain

/əʊ/: coast

Exercise 7

1 spotting

2 rainforests

3 species

4 park

5 jungle

6 cliffs

7 scenery

8 trees

9 nature

10 trekking

11 pond

12 insect

Exercise 8

Mammals: bats, deer, (clouded) leopards, monkeys, orangutans, rhinoceros

Insects and spiders: leeches, sandflies, tarantula

Reptiles and amphibians: (flying) frogs, snakes

PROFESSIONAL SKILLS, PAGE 30

Exercise 1

Water sports: canoeing, scuba diving, snorkelling

Air activities: ballooning, bungee jumping, flightseeing

Mountain sports: mountain biking, snow boarding, trekking

Wildlife activities: bird watching, horse riding, wildlife spotting

Exercise 2

The correct order is e, h, c, g, f, a, b, d.

Exercise 3

1 skiing, snowboarding, trekking

2 29 (23 on the mainland and six on the islands)

3 basic accommodation / huts

4 minus 20°C

5 winter

6 across the Arctic Circle

Exercise 4

1 e **2** g **3** h **4** f **5** b **6** a, c **7** d

Exercises 5 and 6

1 I'd <u>like</u> to <u>tell</u> you about our <u>beautiful</u> <u>parks</u>. (9 words)

2 <u>Then</u> I'm <u>going</u> to <u>show</u> you some <u>photos</u>. (8 words)

3 You'll <u>see</u> some <u>fantastic</u> <u>scenery</u>. (5 words)

4 <u>As</u> you can <u>see</u>, the <u>scenery's</u> <u>spectacular</u>. (7 words)

5 <u>Now</u>, I'll <u>show</u> you the <u>islands</u>. (6 words)

6 It's <u>best</u> to go <u>skiing</u> in the spring. (8 words)

CASE STUDY, PAGE 31

Exercise 1

1 h **2** a **3** g **4** c **5** b **6** e **7** f **8** d

Exercise 2

1 b **2** a **3** a **4** a **5** b

Exercise 3

a 5 **b** 2 **c** 1 **d** 4 **e** 3

Unit 8

GRAMMAR AND VOCABULARY, PAGE 32

Exercise 1

airport information

baggage reclaim

car park

check-in desks

currency exchange

duty-free shops

meeting point

passport control

Exercise 2

Across	Down
1 customs	**1** cash
3 toilets	**2** trolley
8 elevator	**4** luggage/baggage
9 fare	**5** security
10 baggage/luggage	**6** take
11 gate	**7** arrivals
12 pass	

Exercise 3

How to get to central London by public transport.

Exercise 4

1 ~~downtown~~ central London, ~~transportation~~ transport

2 ~~subway~~ underground

3 ~~one-way~~ single, ~~roundtrip~~ return ticket

4 ~~rental~~ hire, ~~elevator~~ lift

5 ~~sidewalk~~ walkway

6 ticket ~~booth~~ office, ~~lines~~ queues

Exercise 5

1 c **2** a **3** c **4** b **5** c **6** a

Exercise 6

2 shouldn't sit

3 should stretch

4 should pack

5 shouldn't have

6 shouldn't put

Exercise 7

1 should get to the airport

2 can't take drinks through

3 don't have to pay for

4 shouldn't lock their check-in

5 allowed to have one

6 mustn't expire during your visit

7 can buy tax-free items

Exercise 8

Advice: 1, 4

Prohibition: 2, 6

No obligation: 3

Permission: 5, 7

Exercise 9

1 can	**5** can't
2 can't	**6** can't
3 can, can	**7** can't
4 can	

PROFESSIONAL SKILLS, PAGE 34

Exercise 1

1 In the baggage reclaim area.

2 The passenger can't find her luggage.

Exercise 2

1 The Athens flight.

2 An hour ago.

3 The baggage receipt.

4 A black suitcase.

5 Go to carousel 5.

Exercise 3

1 behalf	**5** inconvenience
2 apologize	**6** sorry
3 understand	**7** attention
4 delayed	**8** confidence

Exercise 4

1 how: group 7	**5** sign: group 6
2 date: group 3	**6** eight: group 3
3 clear: group 2	**7** phone: group 1
4 right: group 6	**8** don't: group 1

Exercise 5

1 fair – fare	**7** plain – plane
2 license – licence	**8** their – there
3 know – no	**9** hear – here
4 aloud – allowed	**10** I'll – aisle
5 our – hour	**11** write – right
6 weight – wait	**12** ate – eight

CASE STUDY, PAGE 35

Exercise 1

1 diplomatic	**6** sensitive
2 polite	**7** 500
3 calm	**8** smoking in the toilet
4 demanding	**9** safety
5 voice	**10** inform the police

Exercise 2

1 g **2** a **3** b **4** h **5** c **6** e **7** f **8** d

Unit 9

GRAMMAR AND VOCABULARY, PAGE 36

Exercise 1

1 's written	**5** hasn't met
2 checked	**6** hasn't phoned
3 hasn't inspected	**7** hasn't had
4 's spoken	**8** 's gone up

Exercise 2

1 Have they cleaned the third floor (yet)?

2 Where has he gone?

3 Has she had a break (yet)?

4 Have you counted the hangers (yet)?

5 Has he checked the towels (yet)?

6 Have you washed the towels (yet)?

7 Have you talked to the supervisor (yet)?

8 Has she ironed her uniform (yet)?

Exercise 3

/t/: asked, checked, finished, talked, washed

/d/: cleaned, ironed, phoned, repaired, supervised

/ɪd/: counted, inspected

We use the /ɪd/ ending with regular verbs that end in -d or -t.

Exercise 4

1 elevator	**6** folio
2 closet	**7** lobby
3 cart	**8** restroom
4 rank	**9** faucet
5 parking lot	**10** doorman

Exercise 5

Option B is the best summary.

The length of a refurbishment project is incorrect in summary A (10–12 weeks for a simple project but remodelling and bigger projects can take 4–5 months). Summary B mentions minimizing disruption for guests, and safety, which the expert says comes first.

Exercise 6

The expert mentions points 1, 4, 6, 7, 8.

Exercise 7

1 fittings	**6** interior designer
2 refurbishment	**7** defect
3 coordination	**8** disruption
4 remodelling	**9** operations
5 builder	**10** close down

Exercise 8

1 bed linen; *bleach* goes in group 2

2 cleaning products; *duvet* goes in group 1

3 guest room items; *wardrobe* goes in group 5

4 refurbishment; *chandelier* goes in group 6

5 furniture; *notepad* goes in group 3

6 fittings; *remodel* goes in group 4

Exercise 9

oO: design, extend, restore

Oo: lobby, stylish

oOo: designer, extension, refurbish

Ooo: furniture, renovate

ooOo: innovation, renovation, restoration

PROFESSIONAL SKILLS, PAGE 38

Exercise 1

See audio script on page 51.

Exercise 2

1 c May I have

2 f How was your

3 b I'm sorry to

4 e So the balance

5 a Would you like

6 d We look forward

Exercise 3

1 <u>Good</u> <u>morning</u>. <u>May</u> I <u>have</u> your <u>name</u>, <u>please</u>?

2 <u>How</u> was your <u>stay</u> with us?

3 I'm <u>sorry</u> to <u>hear</u> <u>that</u>. I'm <u>afraid</u> the <u>spa</u> <u>closes</u> at <u>9 p.m.</u>

4 <u>So</u> the <u>balance</u> <u>due</u> is <u>two</u> <u>hundred</u> and <u>seventy</u> <u>four</u> <u>dollars</u>.

5 <u>Would</u> you <u>like</u> me to <u>order</u> you a <u>taxi</u>?

6 We <u>look</u> <u>forward</u> to <u>seeing</u> you <u>again</u>.

The stressed words carry the important information.

Exercise 4

b The hotel has over-charged by $100. The pre-paid amount is $174, not $74, so the balance due is $174, not $274.

CASE STUDY, PAGE 39

Exercise 1

1 c **2** d **3** b **4** a

Exercise 2

A 2, 3 **B** 1 **C** 4

Exercise 3

1 M **2** E **3** T **4** E **5** M **6** T

Exercise 4

Emilio recommends 2, 4 and 6. He also thinks cameras (option 1) are a good idea in public areas but not in guest rooms.

Unit 10

GRAMMAR AND VOCABULARY, PAGE 40

Exercise 1

1 city break   **a** family

2 adventure   **b** retired

3 three-star   **c** student

4 luxury   **d** professional

5 working holiday   **e** older

1 e **2** d **3** a **4** b **5** c

Exercise 2

Across   **Down**

1 sponsor   **2** promote

5 flyer   **3** research

6 communicate   **4** campaign

7 advert   **8** target

9 slogan

10 distribute

Exercise 3

1 d **2** c **3** e **4** a **5** b

Exercise 4

1 book   **7** market/marketing

2 development   **8** relax

3 discoverer   **9** tourist

4 discover   **10** tour

5 enjoyment   **11** travel

6 learner   **12** traveller

Exercise 5

1 China ~~becomes~~ will become

2 correct

3 If Asian economies ~~will~~ continue

4 correct

5 Group tours ~~are~~ will probably be

6 ~~they won't~~ they'll

7 Travel companies ~~won't~~ will have to translate

8 correct

PROFESSIONAL SKILLS, PAGE 42

Exercise 1

1 b **2** c **3** e

Exercise 2

1 b **2** b **3** a **4** d **5** c **6** c **7** d **8** a

Exercises 3 and 4

1 If you <u>take</u> this <u>lovely scarf</u>, I'll <u>give</u> you the <u>lot</u> for <u>75 lira</u>.

2 How <u>much</u> will it <u>be</u> if I <u>buy</u> another <u>dress</u>?

3 If you <u>ask Amanda nicely, perhaps</u> she'll <u>work</u> your <u>shift next weekend</u>.

4 I'll <u>swap</u> with you the <u>following weekend</u> if that <u>helps</u>.

5 If you <u>don't invite all</u> your <u>cousins</u>, I'll <u>agree</u> to a <u>more expensive menu</u>.

6 We'll be <u>able</u> to <u>afford</u> a <u>better menu</u> if your <u>mother</u> <u>doesn't invite all</u> her <u>friends</u>.

7 How <u>much</u> will it <u>cost</u> if we <u>choose menu 4</u> and <u>have</u> <u>110 guests</u>?

8 If you <u>decide</u> on <u>menu 4</u> and <u>110 guests</u>, it'll <u>come</u> to <u>£9,300</u>.

CASE STUDY, PAGE 43

Exercise 1

1 b Mumbai

2 c Moscow

3 a the USA

Exercise 2

1 Bollywood   **6** smile

2 shopper's   **7** shows

3 ethnic   **8** dining

4 board   **9** concept

5 heart

Exercise 3

1 activities   **6** beauty

2 people   **7** money

3 food   **8** nightlife

4 culture   **9** beaches

5 resorts   **10** weather

Exercise 4

Six possible tourism values: adventure activities, history and culture, natural beauty, unspoilt beaches, value for money, warm weather

Exercise 5

1 a **2** b **3** a **4** a **5** b **6** b

Exercise 6

Option b

Option a is too long for a slogan. Option c doesn't mention the tourism values suggested in Exercise 3 and it doesn't sound very catchy.

Pearson Education Limited
Edinburgh Gate
Harlow
Essex CM20 2JE
England
and Associated Companies throughout the world.

www.pearsonelt.com/tourism

© Pearson Education Limited 2013

First published 2013

Tenth impression 2022

ISBN: Workbook +Key/Audio CD Pk
978144723893
Printed and bound by CPI Group (UK) Ltd, Croydon, CR0 4YY

Workbook -Key/Audio CD Pk
9781447923909
Printed and bound by CPI Group (UK) Ltd, Croydon, CR0 4YY

Set in Avenir Light 9.5/12.5pt

Text
Extract 2. adapted from Visit Brussels, http://visitbrussels.be/bitc/front/home/display/lg/en/section/visiteur.do, copyright © 2012 - VISITBRUSSELS - All rights reserved; Extract 9. from 'Cost model: Hotel refurbishment', Building Magazine, Issue 23 (Davis Langdon & Everest 2002), www.building.co.uk. Reproduced with permission of Building Magazine.

In some instances we have been unable to trace the owners of copyright material, and we would appreciate any information that would enable us to do so.

'DK' and the DK 'open book' logo are trade marks of Dorling Kindersley Limited and are used in this publication under licence.

Picture Credits
The publisher would like to thank the following for their kind permission to reproduce their photographs:

(Key: b-bottom; c-centre; l-left; r-right; t-top)

Alamy Images: Adrian Sherratt 18cl, Francisco Martinez 18cr, Henk Meijer 15tl, Iain Masterton 41tr, Peter Adams Photography Ltd 42br, Samyak Kaninde 31cl; **Corbis:** HBSS 20tr, moodboard 9cr, Oliver Rossi 10tr, Paul Souders 13cr, Sergey Gorshkov / Minden Pictures 13c; **DK Images:** 25tr, Nigel Hicks 16tr; **Eyewire:** 8cr; **Fotolia.com:** 13tr, 19tr, 28cr, 12, 14tl, 13, 15tr, 16, 18tl, 17, 19tr, 21, 23tr, 24, 26tl, 25, 27tr, 28, 30tl, 29, 31tr, 32, 34tl, 4, 6tl, 40, 42tl, 41, 43tr, 5, 7tr, 8, 10tl, 9, 11tr; **Getty Images:** Antony Spencer / Vetta 30bl, Comstock 22bl, Lester Lefkowitz 7tl, SJ. Kim 40cr; **Pearson Education Ltd:** Naki Kouyioumtzis 37br; **Rex Features:** Isopix 32tr, Ros Drinkwater 14tr, Sipa Press 4tr, 32br, Sipa Press 4tr, 32br; **Robert Harding World Imagery:** Bill Gozansky / age fotostock 23tr, Eurasia 17br, Roy Rainford 5tl, 12c; **Shutterstock.com:** 19tc, 20, 22tl, 33, 35tr, 36, 38tl, 37, 39tr; **SuperStock:** 7bl, age fotostock 27tr, Cusp 38tr

Cover images: Front: **4Corners Images:** Benedetta Rusconi / SIME t; **Corbis:** F.Stuart Westmorland b, Jon Hicks bc; **SuperStock:** Fancy Collection tc

All other images © Pearson Education

In some instances we have been unable to trace the owners of copyright material, and we would appreciate any information that would enable us to do so.